ERNEST SHACKLETON

Biography®

ERNEST SHACKLETON

George Plimpton

LONDON, NEW YORK, MUNICH,
MELBOURNE, and DELHI

DK PUBLISHING
Publisher Chuck Lang
Creative Director Tina Vaughan
Editorial Director Chuck Wills
Art Director Dirk Kaufman
Production Manager Chris Avgherinos
DTP Designer Milos Orlovic

First American Edition, 2003
2 4 6 8 10 9 7 5 3 1
Published in the United States
by DK Publishing, Inc.
375 Hudson Street
New York, New York 10014

produced by AVALON PUBLISHING GROUP, INC.
Project Editor Max Alexander
Senior Director, Editorial Will Balliett
Senior Director, Operations f-stop Fitzgerald
Photo Editor Tracy Armstead
Designer Lisa Vaughn-Soraghan
Assistant Editor Kristen Couse
Production Manager Mike Walters
Production Editor Simon Sullivan

A&E TELEVISION NETWORK
Director of Licensing Carrie Trimmer
Director Legal & Business Affairs Chey Blake
VP/GM Consumer Products & Merchandising Steve Ronson

Photo Credits—See page 152

DK Publishing, Inc. offers special discounts for bulk purchases for
sales promotions or premiums. Specific, large-quantity needs can be
met with special editions, including personalized covers, excerpts of
existing guides, and corporate imprints. For more information,
contact Special Markets Department, DK Publishing, Inc.,
375 Hudson Street, New York, NY 10014 Fax: 212-689-5254.

Cataloging-in-Publication data is available from
the Library of Congress

ISBN 0-7894-9315-2

Reproduced by ColourScan, Singapore.
Printed and bound by R. R. Donnelley in the United States.

See our complete product line at
www.dk.com

Contents

6
Foreword

11
Southward Bound 1874–1903

29
The *Nimrod* Sails 1904–1909

47
South Georgia 1910–1914

61
On the Ice
December 1914–April 1916

89
The Voyage of the *James Caird*
April–May 1916

99
Crossing the Mountains
May 19-20, 1916

111
Elephant Island
April–October 1916

125
Aurora 1914–1916

141
Quest 1917–1922

152
Photo Credits, Index, & Acknowledgements

Foreword

I can't recall when I first heard Sir Ernest Shackleton's name, but it was very likely in school, probably in connection with Robert Falcon Scott. Scott was an early hero. When I was eleven or twelve I read a lot about him, compelled among other things by that perfect, utterly romantic, middle name. Falcon. I craved that name for myself, either as a given or family name, perhaps both. Falcon Falcon, explorer, baseball player, whatever. His failure to reach the South Pole before Roald Amundsen in 1911 was heart-rending as I read about it, and even more so his death with Henry Bowers and Edward Wilson in the blizzard-torn tent on the return trip. Captain Oates and Edgar Evans were with them, and died before that last encampment; Oates's words as he walked out of the tent into the blizzard (on his birthday, what's more!) were engraved in my memory. "I am just going outside and I may be some time." I often repeated those words leaving a schoolmate's room, and even today, walking out on a noisy cocktail party, I find myself saying them under my breath.

Shackleton was not on that ill-fated trip. But he was with Scott on the *Discovery* expedition in 1902, their first to the Antarctic. Both men were friends at the start, but became rivals, their lives as explorers intertwined. Both were competitive to a degree: that year, 1902, both went up one after the other in a tethered balloon to survey the Ross Ice Shelf. Scott went first, but Shackleton on his ascent made a point of going higher. I don't remember reading about this in my schoolboy days, but I surely would have been upset at Shackleton for doing such a thing...showing up my childhood hero. Besides, Shackleton's middle name is Henry—hardly a candleflame's worth next to Falcon!

Then years went by, into adulthood, without my thinking very much more about Scott, much less Shackleton, until in 1997 a young woman named Caroline Alexander wrote a short book named *Mrs. Chippy, Last Expedition*—a charming diary purportedly written by the cat (she turned out to be a male) aboard Shackleton's ship, *Endurance*. The book's jacket showed the cat, a gray and white tiger, perched

First Timer
A photograph of Shackleton taken at Cape Adare on January 9, 1902 just after he came ashore from Robert Falcon Scott's *Discovery*— the explorer's first steps on the Antarctic continent.

next to crew member Percy Blackborrow's neck with his paws down on the young man's shoulder blades. Blackborrow had crept on board *Endurance* in Buenos Aires as a stowaway.

The success of the book helped rekindle interest in Shackleton, as did a nationwide tour in 2000 (her book *Endurance* was published at the same time) of Frank Hurley's remarkable photographs of the *Endurance* expedition, which Caroline Alexander had rediscovered on a dusty shelf in a back storeroom of the Royal Geographic Society in London. Also in the exhibit was the original whaleboat, *James Caird*, in which Shackleton and five shipmates had sailed over 800 miles from Elephant Island to South Georgia in their attempt to get help for those left behind—a voyage considered one of the great exploits of the heroic age of exploration.

About that time I was at work on a book about bird-watching (a long time hobby perhaps induced by Scott's middle name) in which some of the chapters involved looking for rare birds around the world—the Congo peacock in the eastern reaches of the Congo, first identified in 1924, and the imperial ivory-billed woodpecker in the Northern pine forests of Mexico. Perhaps saw the first skulking in the rain forest undergrowth, no luck with the woodpecker (as large as a raven!), which is almost surely extinct. It was last seen in 1954.

Finalists

Henry Bowers (seated left, next to Edward Wilson) set up this melancholic photograph of Robert Scott's party at the South Pole on January 17, 1912. Their faces reflect acute physical suffering, as well as plain disappointment over losing the race. Standing, left to right, are Laurence Oates, Scott, and Edgar Evans. All five died on the return trek.

Asked to do a book on Shackleton, it occurred to me that in the course of visiting the places made famous by Shackleton's expedition, I could keep an eye out for interesting birds—the emperor penguin, the largest of its species, a small bird named the South Georgia pipit, very rare, a large raptor, the striated caracara, and a bird I'd read about in a travel brochure—a meat-eating carnivorous duck indigenous to the area.

Through the good graces of an old friend, George Butler, who produced and directed the IMAX-format film *Shackleton's Antarctic Adventure*, I was able to secure a berth aboard the Russian icebreaker *Kapitan Dranitsyn,* scheduled to travel to South Georgia, then in the Weddell Sea to the Peninsula and Elephant Island.

At the last, however, the ship's itinerary was changed, leaving out South Georgia—an essential stop for me since it was not only the base from which Shackleton set out to try to cross the Antarctic continent but to which he returned on the *James Caird*. His traverse of the mid-island mountain range laced with glaciers to get to the whaling station at Stromness and safety is considered one of the most extraordinary feats of mountaineering history. And, of course, South Georgia is the home of, perhaps, the mysterious carnivorous duck.

Fortunately I was able to secure a berth aboard the *Explorer,* a small cruise ship approved by the Abercrombie & Kent travel organization. I had been on her once before on a birding expedition to the Amazon. The itinerary included not only South Georgia and Elephant Island, but the Falklands as well, with its rich bird life.

Home Base
Abercrombie & Kent's cruise ship *Explorer*, known as "The Little Red Ship" for her striking lines. Commissioned by Lindblad, she was the first purpose-built passenger ship to visit the Antarctic continent, in 1970.

So what follows is an account of Shackleton's life and four expeditions to the south, cross-hatched with some of my own impressions. As almost all the principals who were with Shackleton kept diaries, it seemed appropriate enough for me to keep a kind of journal. Fortunately, the *Explorer's* library was extensive, shelves of books pertinent to the expedition—travel, exploration, bird guides, biographies—among them Shackleton's *South* and Roland Huntford's extensive biography *Shackleton*. Aboard *Explorer* there were daily lectures on any number of topics relative to our trip—whaling, the principal characters of Antarctic exploration, the fauna, and there was one simply titled "Ice". Some of the entries in the journal came later, of course, as I picked up additional information, some of it germane, some not, which is the pleasure of facing a blank page. Why not start with a poem?

Endurance

Once upon a time, *began the old tale,*
and that's how we knew it was a tale. Shackleton's
fare-thee-well voyage, ship marooned in ice

until the hull cracked like matchsticks,
crew booting a soccer ball across the shelf.
The photographer tilted his flash pots to catch

hoarfrost on the rigging. We splay our fingers
over their mute images, a century later,
knowing their fate as they could not,

as others will know our fates, though we cannot.
More tragicomedy than tragedy, unlike Franklin[1]
starving with his crew, Hudson[2] *and his boy adrift.*

The men of the Endurance, crossing at the worst season,
low on provision, landfall on a desolate island
at a forgotten whaling station, Shackleton

pressing on, the stumpy ketch a scar in crosshatched sea,
the captain's sun-sighting through muffled cloud
a feat of reckoning judged greater than Bligh's.[3]

And still an ice mountain to traverse with frayed rope,
months twiddling their thumbs to rescue the men,
the heroism not presence of virtue, or absence of vanity.

—William Logan, January 18, 2002

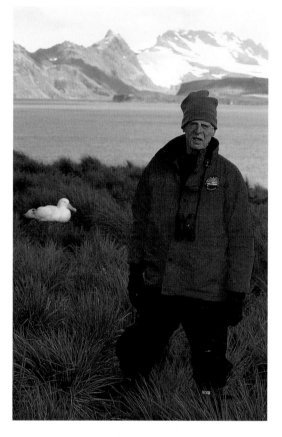

South Georgia
The author stands against a background of the mountains of South Georgia, in the foreground an unperturbed wandering albatross, settled on its tussock nest.

Notes on the poem can be found on page 154.

Southward Bound
1874–1903

I had some books in my bag on the flight coming down to Santiago, Chile, for the flight across to the Falkland Islands to board the *Explorer*. Among them was Apsley Cherry-Garrard's book *The Worst Journey in the World*, which I was to find the most instructive and entertaining of all the books on the Antarctic. Cherry-Garrard, who had accompanied Scott in the first stages of his fatal expedition in 1912, was pushed to write the book by George Bernard Shaw and resisted for a while because he felt himself too much the amateur to do such a thing. Chatty and breezy, this book begins with one of the great opening lines of exploration literature: "Polar exploration is at once the cleanest and most isolated way of having a bad time which has been devised."

I had to put the book aside because very little turned up in it about Shackleton. I did read enough on the flight to realize Cherry-Garrard thought very little of the polar explorations of the time. He writes: "It is amazing to one who looks back upon these first efforts of the *Discovery* expedition [Scott's first to the Antarctic with Shackleton aboard] that the results were not more disastrous than was actually the case. When one reads of dog-teams which refused to start, of Pemmican [a dried meat preparation] which was considered too rich to eat, of two officers discussing the ascent of Erebus and back in one day, and of sledging parties which knew not how to use their cookers or lamps, nor even how to put on their clothes, then one begins to wonder that the process of education was gained at so small a price."

So having read a paragraph or two chivvying away the accomplishments of my favorite boyhood hero, Scott, I looked elsewhere in my reading material to get a sense of Shackleton. The photographs show a slightly jutting jaw, wide mouth, a prominent nose, and hair parted in the middle. I came across a photograph showing Shackleton and Scott on skis, Shackleton in a broad hat looking in dress very much like a gold prospector in the American West, Scott in a sweater, stiff collar, and tie. Both are carrying a single ski pole, which was how one often skied cross-country in those days. Both look quite ill at ease.

Shackleton was born on February 15, 1874, in Kilkea, County Kildare, Ireland (he liked to say that he shared his birthday with Galileo), to Protestant parents of English descent. He lived briefly in Dublin, and was educated at home until he was eleven and a half by a governess. In 1884, his parents (his father was a doctor) moved their family permanently to London. His father sent him to Dulwich College, a middle-class private institution—what the British call a public school—in the hopes that he would move on from there into a medical career. But he was an unremarkable student, bored in the classroom and bad at team sports. Though he did, however, earn a reputation as a persuasive speaker. While he very much wanted a naval career, his father could not afford cadet training. Instead, young Shackleton, perhaps because he had eight sisters, joined the merchant marine and went to sea. He was sixteen.

With the help of family connections he was able to ship out on the *Hoghton Tower*, a square-rigger, just about the last of such ships before steam took over. He went five times around Cape Horn, the storm-wracked tip of South America that was the only water passage between the Atlantic and the Pacific. (The Panama Canal, though under construction, was not completed until 1914). On one occasion the *Hoghton Tower* encountered head winds that held the ship up, bucking around in heavy seas, for two months. There must have been times on those troubled trips around the Horn when Shackleton looked south and persuaded himself that a life of adventure and polar exploration lay ahead.

In August, 1894, he took his examination for second mate, then spent five years on the tramp steamer *Monmouthshire*. In 1898, he was certified as master, which meant that he could command any British ship on the seas. He was twenty-four.

On a shore leave from the merchant marine in 1897, Shackleton had met one of

Big Family

Shackleton (center, rear) poses with his eight sisters and (seated in front) his younger brother, Frank, in a late 19th-century family portrait. Ernest was the second oldest of the clan.

DISCOVERING ANTARCTICA

It would be hard to overstate the fascination for Antarctic exploration in Shackleton's time. Most parts of Africa, Asia, and South America had been walked on or mapped. Yet there existed a continent larger than Europe or the United States whose population was nil. Men who set off to discover this land were celebrated as heroes. The earliest was Captain James Cook, who went around Antarctica in the 1770s but saw no land. About fifty years later a Russian, Fabian von Bellinghausen, glimpsed mountains in the distance from his ship, thus confirming that land lay beneath the snow and ice. After that, many U.S. and British sealers saw and mapped the continent, very

This engraving of Captain James Cook by William Holl II is based on a painting by Nathaniel Dance. Cook, who was murdered in the Sandwich Islands in 1779, was the most famous explorer of the 18th century.

likely some of them going ashore. The first who publicized setting foot on the continent was a member of a Norwegian sealing and whaling expedition in 1894 on the *Antarctic,* an assistant biologist named Carsten Borchgrevink. The captain, named Leonard Kristensen, later claimed *he* was first. In actual fact, the first was very likely a young boy named Alexander Tunzleman who got off the boat to steady it so that the captain (or Borchgrevink) could disembark.

THE FROZEN DESERT

Antarctica, the fifth largest continent, is covered by a layer of ice so vast that, if it were to melt, the world's oceans would rise by two hundred feet. It is in fact ninety percent of the world's ice and sixty-eight percent of its fresh water. Over some of Antarctica's deepest rock basins, the ice is 15,000 feet deep.

Oddly, for all that frozen water, which took millions of years to build up, Antarctica is a relative desert, the driest continent on Earth due to extreme cold and low humidity. The very slight precipitation falls in the form of ice crystals, sometimes called

Antarctica's lonely beauty belies a savage environment that demands respect—and offers no forgiveness to those who fail to prepare.

diamond dust, which often falls out of a clear sky and can create spectacular refractions of the sun and moon.

Antarctica is also the most mountainous of the continents, with an average elevation of 8,000 feet. Its tallest peak, 16,860-foot Vinson Massif, is named after a U.S. congressman, Carl G. Vinson, who was a main supporter of American polar exploration during his fifty years in office.

his sister's friends, Emily Dorman, a tall dark-haired woman six years his senior. He fell very much in love with her. The following year, his ship, the *Flintshire,* ran aground on the English coast within traveling distance, and a twenty-four hour leave gave Shackleton a chance to visit her in London. It was a memorable visit. She described it in a letter: "We spent the evening in the billiard room—he told me how he loved me—I was deeply moved— I remember so well—because he put his cigarette on a ledge in the big oak chimney piece—& it burnt a deep dent— which we tried to rub out—and we often looked at it in after days—but no one else noticed it!"

It was fortunate Dorman Sr. never noticed, because he didn't approve of his future son-in-law at all, especially the young man's wandering lifestyle. His daughter was of a different mind. She wrote later, "I never wittingly hampered his ardent spirit, or tried to chain it to the domestic life that meant so much to me." An inherited trust of £700 per year would later allow her to maintain a household and their three children (Raymond, Emily, and Edward, later Lord Shackleton) while her husband was away.

At the end of May 1900, Shackleton read a report in the *Times* of London that the National Antarctic Expedition, long in the planning, was to be commanded by Robert Falcon Scott. Sir Clements Markham, who at the time was the president of the Royal Geographical Society, had picked Scott. Among other reasons, Markham had chosen Scott because he'd appreciated his competitiveness winning a boat race, and was also struck by "his intelligence, information, and charm of manner."

Roland Huntford, in his biography, *Shackleton,* takes issue. I was discouraged to read that Scott was rather dull and conventional, that he lacked one of the essential qualities of leadership: running a happy ship. He was something of a bully, panicky in moments of stress. And he had utterly no skills or experience at polar exploration. He concludes, "Today, it seems inconceivable that anyone so blatantly unprepared would be chosen to lead a British national enterprise."

I grunted slightly, and went on to read that Shackleton, quite unaware of this, volunteered for the National Antarctic Expedition. He went to meet

Ernest and Emily
This 1910 photograph shows Shackleton and wife Emily situated in his favorite milieu— aboard a ship—and far from her chosen life in a quiet country home. They never reconciled this basic difference.

Scott in London, who was impressed enough to hire him to work in the expedition's offices. He was, in a sense, well qualified—energetic, endowed with the easy charm of a good salesman, strong-minded (he took passionate stands against alcohol—a stance which gave way in later life), opportunistic, and, of course, with years of experience at sea. He was also impatient and must have been pleased when Scott put him in charge of the sea trials of the expedition ship, *Discovery,* after the launching in March 1901.

In August of that year, Scott set sail with Shackleton aboard. *Discovery* was one of the last wooden ships of her kind built in Britain—the choice of wood because it was more elastic than steel and thus not as prone to cracking and breaking from the crush of ice. She had steam auxiliary engines that used coal as fuel, but was truly a sailing ship refitted as a barque—three-masted with square rigging on the fore and main masts.

From the trip south, an interesting portrait of Shackleton emerges. The librarian of the Royal Geographic Society, Hugh Robert Mill, who wrote a biography of Shackleton, was on board. He described Shackleton's astonishing powers of memory: "I always associate Shackleton with the starlight of a summer night in the Bay of Biscay. I had known him for a year before, but it was on the bridge of the *Discovery* from midnight on, as the ship was rolling southward that I discovered his individuality and recognized how he differed in turn of phrase and trend of mind from the other splendid fellows on board for an early stage of the trip. To tell the truth, I was at first surprised and a little alarmed at the ceaseless flow of quotation from the poets called forth by the summer night, the stars, the phosphorescence of the sea, and the thought of those he left behind him. Nor was it altogether pleasant to find that this young sailor was already familiar with every reference which rose to my mind from books I had read years before his thoughts had turned that way, and with many which I had never seen."

Also on board was Dr. Edward A. Wilson, a Cambridge University graduate, a talented artist, deeply religious, and Shackleton's best friend on the expedition. He wrote his wife, "Shackleton's conversation is sparkling and witty to a high degree. He has a wonderful memory, and has an amazing treasure of most interesting anecdote. That and his quick wit and keen humour are his strong point at table." Wilson also wrote about Shackleton's absorption with poetry, with just a hint that perhaps it was excessive: "He knows

Stiff Upper Lip
Robert Falcon Scott was considered a stern and humorless leader, as this rather severe portrait suggests. Even so, he personified British resolve, which helps explain his popularity.

nearly every bit of poetry that has ever been written and is always ready to quote it ... "

Wilson held a number of positions. He was the expedition's junior surgeon and also a biologist, an artist in the ornithological field of great distinction. Thin, tall, red-haired, intense, very much the scientist, he hoped to collect the eggs of the emperor penguin at Cape Crozier on Ross Island off the Ross Ice Shelf. As for Shackleton, he was not much of a bird man. In his diary Wilson reports that Shackleton told his men "that all you had to do to get the penguin to lay was to throttle it and the egg would fall out."

✧ ✧ ✧

JOURNAL ENTRY, 2002 • *The Falklands*
From Santiago we arrived in the Falklands, a British dependency, landing at Mount Pleasant airport. Two field guns on the tarmac, and a plaque dedicated by Prince Andrew who was on duty there, flying a Royal Air Force plane off a carrier in the Falklands War. Two hundred herds of sheep. We saw some of these during an hour bus drive to Stanley across the barren, somewhat rolling terrain, passing an occasional minefield with a skull-and-crossbones sign to mark its location. The mines, planted by the Argentinians during the war, are made of plastic, and can bear the weight of an occasional lamb walking over them, apparently, but not a human. Twenty-two pounds will set them off. There are 20,000-odd mines around Stanley. Not counting the military based at Mount Pleasant, the Falklands population is about 2,000, half of whom live in Stanley. We are told all this by a guide standing in the front well of the bus, a pleasant gent, who at the time of the war in 1982—referred to around here as "The Conflict"—was a policeman, very likely the only one in town, and was locked up in his own jail when the Argentinians invaded.

Stanley. Odd, not a townsperson to be seen ... as if a gas had wiped them out. The only trees on the island are here. The natives call themselves "kelpers," referring to the rich kelp beds that encircle the islands. I don't know this for a fact since I never met anyone to ask. Some of the houses have large stones on the roofs to keep a strong wind from lifting them off, like a lid from a pot.

Young Adventurer
In contrast to Scott's icy stare, Shackleton projected a more easygoing demeanor. Even this rather formal portrait hints at his relaxed charm.

✧ ✧ ✧

Balloon Trip

Edward Wilson was scheduled to go up in the third balloon ascent but declined. He found the whole exercise "lunatic." Unintentionally critiquing much of early polar exploration, he wrote: "I think it is perfect madness to allow novices to risk their lives in this silly way." The masts of *Discovery*, moored at the base of the ice shelf, are visible in the background.

Discovery's departure from New Zealand on Christmas Eve 1901 was marked by misfortune. As she left Lyttleton Harbor with smaller craft following along, horns blaring, a seaman named Bonner climbed to the crow's nest to watch the celebratory proceedings and lost his balance when the first of the sea swells rocked the ship: he fell to his death on the deckhouse clutching the weathervane from the masthead that he had been hanging on to for support and which had given way. Superstitious sailors were affected by this, and were doubly troubled when Frank Wild, who was later to become closely identified with Shackleton, shot an albatross, a bird attached to the fortunes of a voyage, as one knew from Coleridge's "Rime of the Ancient Mariner."

On January 22, 1902, *Discovery* arrived at the Ross Ice Shelf, at the southernmost reach of the Pacific Ocean—a wall of ice, mast high, often higher, that runs along the coast of Antarctica for 400 miles. It was thought at the time (the theory of the Norwegian Carsten Borchgrevink) that the top of the shelf was smooth and level and ran that way clear south to the horizon and most likely to the Pole. This gave the impression that the 1,600-mile trip there and back might be a relatively easy jaunt. Scott found a good landing spot at McMurdo Sound, a relatively sheltered inlet thirty miles across and thirty miles in length, tucked in behind mountainous Ross Island, which was dominated by the active volcano Erebus.

Where the ice shelf at one place sloped down to the water like a ramp, he landed and immediately put up a balloon attached to a thin cable to check Borchgrevink's theory. The balloon's skin was made of cow gut, the gas bag filled with hydrogen from cylinders, a small wicker basket dangling underneath. Scott went up first so that, as he admitted frankly, he would have the honor of being the continent's first aeronaut. Shackleton went up

next. The balloon rose over 650 feet, and he at least had the satisfaction of taking the first aerial photographs of Antarctica. They showed what Borchgrevink had suggested—an expanse of snowfields stretching out unimpeded to the south.

Following the balloon ascent, Scott sailed down the length of McMurdo Sound to a bay behind a promontory where, very close to the Ross Ice Shelf, *Discovery* was secured for the winter.

On shore, Scott built what became called the Hut, later an important landmark in Antarctic exploration. Originally it was used as a storehouse and a place of shelter if there was an emergency, such as a fire on board the ship. Scott then had his people set up a large tent to house everybody in case the Hut caught fire … a suggestion that at least in some cases, Scott was a very prudent leader.

They spent the winter encased in ice and darkness—the only light the faint glow against the clouds from the crater of Mt. Erebus.

✧　　✧　　✧

JOURNAL ENTRY, 2002 • *Sea Lion Island, Falklands*
We went ashore from the *Explorer* and Greg Lasley, the tour's bird expert, and I went out along the coastline to see what was around. I asked him about the carnivorous duck. He looked horrified. "Come on, now," he said.

"I read about it," I insisted.

"You mean it *attacks* and all that?" He shook his head.

I replied lamely that my sister had seen a brown thrasher (a member of the thrush family) eat a shrew.

Greg shook his head again. He doubtless thinks that I too believe, with Shackleton, that by throttling a penguin, an egg will drop out.

At least as interesting is a Falkland bird we saw called the flightless steamer duck, so named because it leaves a trail behind it in calm water like a paddle steamer's as it tries desperately to take off but can't. It tries for fifty yards or so,

YELLOW FEVER

February, 1902
• Two United States Army physicians determine that the deadly tropical disease known as yellow fever is transmitted by mosquitoes. Walter Reed and James Carroll publish a scientific report based on their studies of the disease in Havana, Cuba.

Ice Field
Scott's *Discovery* enters the pack ice guarding the Ross Sea. A fellow explorer, Otto Nordenskjold, wrote of this: "Slowly the vessel glides ahead while both sides scrape against the ice with a long, drawn-out roar that deceptively reminds one of the rumbling of thunder…there reigned a desolation and wildness which, perhaps, no other place on Earth could show. I experienced a sense of helplessness as if standing alone and deserted amidst mighty natural forces."

and then coasts to a stop and looks flustered. I asked Greg if the flightless steamer duck could possibly be the carnivorous duck I'd heard tell of. He looked at me and once again shook his head dismissively.

To our surprise, late in the afternoon we saw the striated caracara sitting on a fence post—big and hawk-like, with an odd-looking tumor sticking out of the feathers of its chest. Both Greg and I thought the bird was ill, not far from toppling lifeless off the fence post. It turned out that it was the bird's crop, swollen, a rather ugly feature. The parents drive them off the nests as young adults. The youngsters then collect together and behave rather like teenage gangs, swooping down on a tent whose occupants have gone off on a hike, for example, and rummaging about—making off with rolls of toilet paper and toothpaste tubes, ripping apart pillows, and indeed (in a film I saw about them), pulling out the tent pins so the whole thing collapses in a billowy heap.

The tussock bird. Surely the most inquisitive of birds, it hops about, the size of a ping-pong ball: a man sleeping it off in the Falklands will awake to find the tussock bird walking up his stomach, and feel the slight itch of its tiny claws, as it comes up to inspect his whiskers.

The bird is named after the tussock grass plant that is everywhere in the sub-Antarctic. Tussock, from the word meaning "mound," grows on itself, on the pedestal of its forebears, so that a single plant, 200 years old, can stand two feet on its thirteen-foot tall mound. The strong winds move across this thick carpet and make it seem alive with motion, like a botanical sea.

✧　✧　✧

Upon setting up winter quarters, Scott announced to the company that in the summer he would attempt to reach the Pole. He sent Shackleton on a scouting expedition to the south with two others, Wilson (who was known by the ship's company as "Bill" or "Uncle Bill"), and Hartley Ferrar, also a Cambridge graduate, a good athlete (he rowed for his college), the youngest in the wardroom at twenty-two.

The three had a miserable time of it, largely of their own making. They couldn't ski, obviously the best way to get through the deep snow, and they didn't bring any of the sled dogs that Scott had taken, if reluctantly, along on the ship. He shared the British explorers' perverse aversion to the use of dogs, feeling that was a kind of cheating. Scott had once wrote, "No journey made with dogs can approach the sublimity of a party of men who succeed by their own unaided efforts."

The Striated Caracara
A dark hawk-like bird, rare in the sense that it is only found in the Falklands and islands in the vicinity of Cape Horn. Locally known as "Johnny Rook," the striated caracara is quite a nuisance. Not only do they terrorize the penguin and shag colonies, but I was told of one that cultivated the habit of picking rubber off windshield wipers. This one is sitting on a massive tussock clump.

Other problems ensued. The three men had never set up a tent before. They had a hard time lighting the Primus stove. Their clothing and footwear were inadequate. In four days they managed only a few miles and the ascent of a hillock called a *nunatak*, an Eskimo word for an outcropping of rock through the ice. Their reconnaissance had been somewhat of a failure, but of the three it had given them valuable experience in the snows. Scott picked Shackleton and Wilson to go with him that summer.

On November 2 Scott's little group began the trek south onto the Ross Ice Shelf, into what Shackleton described as a "weird white world." The three had skis but were awkward in their use. One problem was that their skis were soaked in linseed oil, fine for downhill and slaloms, but not for purchase on the snow: the ski simply slides back and forth.

They had the good sense to bring the dogs this time, nineteen of them to begin with, but made the mistake of harnessing them as a single unit, all in a line, rather than dividing them into a number of teams, each pulling its own sledge. They didn't appreciate that a team will move better if it has a lead dog. They never figured out that dog teams work best at the trot, and that the handlers can slide on skis alongside . . . or tricks like shaking the sled slightly when starting off, making it seem "alive" so the dogs don't feel they are pulling a deadweight. The work with the overloaded dogs went so badly that even in the best of conditions one day's effort was only two and a half miles. So a kind of leapfrog advance was initiated: a team would move forward with supplies, set up a depot, and then double back to bring the rest of the gear

Explorer's Cup

A hot cup of "hoosh" was a welcome meal on Antarctica. This cup, from the Discovery expedition, is emblazoned with the logo of a penguin.

Royal Hut?

Britain's Princess Anne inspecting the interior of the *Discovery* hut at McMurdo Sound in February 2002. Scott insisted that Shackleton avoid the hut on his 1907 *Nimrod* expedition.

THE ROSS ICE SHELF

Sir James Ross, on seeing the 400-mile long ice shelf that was eventually named after him, wrote: "It presented an extraordinary appearance, gradually increasing in height as we got nearer to it, and proving at length to be a perpendicular cliff of ice, between one hundred and fifty and two hundred feet above the sea, perfectly flat at the top and without any fissure or promontories on its seaward face … we might as well try to sail through the cliffs of Dover as to penetrate such a mass."

The shelf is "fed" by vast glaciers running down from the mountains. This constant movement of ice pushes the shelf further out to sea, where it eventually

Sledging on the Shelf, wrote *Aurora* expedition member R.W. Richard, "is interrupted very frequently by violent blizzards, when the usual practice was to lay up in the tents and cut to half rations. During a bad blizzard it as inadvisable to leave the tent for any purpose at all."

loses stability and breaks apart. In October 1987, a tabular iceberg, named rather clinically B-9, broke off the Ross Ice Shelf, taking with it a great slab about the size of Long Island. It was tracked for two years by satellites and aircraft until it finally broke into three pieces. One fascinating statistic was that B-9's bulk carried enough fresh water to provide everyone on the planet with two glasses per day for 1,977 years.

forward. Thus a day's journey was only a third of what it could have been if the entire team had moved forward as one.

The three knew so little about the effect of the weather, and worried that it would turn on them, that they often stopped for the day and pitched their tent when they could have continued for additional miles. Once settled, the usual practice was to read aloud to each other. Shackleton had brought along Thomas Huxley's *Lay Sermons* and the poems of Robert Browning, the love of whose work he shared with Emily. Wilson, who had aspirations in an earlier time to become a clergyman, read from the Bible. On Sundays, propped up on a pillow at the end of his sleeping bag, he conducted a sort of Sunday service, reading the psalms and gospels appropriate to that particular date. His congregation of two could hardly be considered staunch members of the faithful. Scott had brought along Darwin's *Origin of Species*, almost as a challenge, it would seem, and read parts of it back to Wilson once the Sunday service was over.

Tempers began to flare. Scott blew up at Shackleton for accidentally knocking over the Primus stove and burning a hole in the tent's ground sheet. His exasperation grew to such a pitch that he peevishly decided they should turn back. Wilson had to argue him out of it—pretty much on the grounds that they had covered such an insignificant distance that the public's dismay and scorn would have no bounds once they got back to England.

But the tension between Scott and Shackleton increased. Scott developed an increasing dislike for Shackleton—perhaps a visceral reaction to his more outgoing personality, and a bit of snobbery, as Royal Navy officers often felt toward men from the merchant marine. Shackleton, meanwhile, had by now lost respect for Scott, whom he considered an ineffective and tyrannical leader. Official protocol was much looser in the merchant marine than in the navy, and Shackleton was appalled by Scott's rigid and humorless style. It had all the makings of a serious confrontation—which very nearly happened a few days later, after Scott called Shackleton a "bloody fool."

Shackleton replied, "You are the worst bloody fool of the lot, and every time you dare to speak to me like that you will get it back." Scott went into a rage, and again threatened to turn back. Wilson calmed him down, but any bond between Scott and Shackleton had been irretrievably broken.

Middle Man

Even-tempered Edward Wilson (below, with one of the ponies from the *Terra Nova* expedition) was usually the peacemaker in the quarrels between Scott and Shackleton during the Furthest South journey.

Furthest South

Scott, Shackleton, and Wilson break for a self-portrait on their polar trek. Of the three, Shackleton was the only one who would never see the Pole; the other two died after reaching it a decade later.

Yet another problem with the trio was that none of them was in the best physical condition. Scott had stomach problems. Wilson not only had been ill with tuberculosis but frequently endured snow blindness, a very painful condition in which the cornea is sunburned through overexposure; he suffered this on a number of occasions when he took off his goggles to make sketches. He trudged along blindfolded, day-dreaming of walking in the woods of England. "Some times I was in beech woods, sometimes in fir woods, sometimes in the Birdlip woods…in the hot sun…and the swish-swish of the ski was as though one's feet were brushing through dead leaves, or cranberry undergrowth or heather or juicy bluebells. One could almost see and smell them."

As for Shackleton, he had a rickety heart—how serious was unclear, because he avoided doctors, but bad enough to cause palpitations. A heavy smoker and a probable asthmatic, he coughed frequently, much to the annoyance of the others at night in their tent. All of them, not long into the trip, began to show signs of scurvy—lethargy, pain in the extremities, bleeding gums.

Because Scott had not made plans to ration food from the start, all began to suffer hunger pangs. Shackleton wrote of this: "We always dream of something to eat when asleep. My general dream is that fine three-cornered tarts are flying past me, but I never seem to stop them. Billy [Wilson] dreams he is cutting sandwiches for somebody else always. The Captain—lucky man—thinks he is eating stuff, but the joy only lasts in the dreams for he is just as hungry when he wakes up."

Wilson in his diary doesn't mention the sandwich dream but he writes of another: "Dreams as a rule of splendid food, ball suppers, sirloins of beef, cauldrons full of steaming vegetables. But one spends all one's time

shouting at waiters who won't bring one a plate of anything, or else one finds the beef is only ashes when one gets it."

Malnutrition also began to affect the dogs. Their canned fishmeal from Norway (purchased eighteen months before) was green with mold. Finally, the dogs began to die off. By the 20th of December, seven weeks out, fourteen were left of the original nineteen.

At the 81st parallel, which they reached on December 15, Scott realized that they had no hope of reaching the pole and proposed that they make a dash to get the Furthest South record, a mark he set at the 82nd parallel, killing the weaker dogs on the way to feed the stronger. They weren't even prepared to do this properly. Wilson had to kill the dogs with a scalpel from his medical kit. On one occasion when Wilson was snowblind, Shackleton had to substitute for him. He notes, "Got his heart first time," then adds the vivid detail that when he tried to carve up the dog it began to sink from the pressure of his carving into the soft snow.

They finally reached the point 82 degrees and 17 minutes—some 270 miles from their base at Hut Point and 745 miles from the pole, at which Scott reluctantly gave the order to turn back. The dogs were down to only five and while they were capable of pulling a load, it wasn't considered, and they simply ran alongside the sledge, often in front of it, while the men strained at the traces, pulling the sledge as if it were a big rickshaw. On January 15, the last two dogs were killed—"utterly useless," according to Wilson.

Of the three Shackleton had become the weakest, victimized by scurvy (blackened gums, spitting blood, legs affected), so weak that even pumping the Primus stove left him panting as if he'd run a fast mile. In the latter stages of the return journey he was so weak that he had to suffer the ignominy of lying on the sledge and being hauled along by the other two,

PRESIDENT ROOSEVELT

July 4, 1903
• On Independence Day, President Theodore Roosevelt sends the first round-the world cable. His message from New York to the Philippines is carried over the new Pacific Cable, where a reply continues around the world and across the Atlantic, back to New York. Total time: 9.5 minutes.

SCURVY

In medical terms, scurvy is known as a "deficiency" disease, caused by a lack of vitamin C in the diet. It is characterized at first by depression and an increasing failure of resolve, followed by muscular weakness, blackened gums, teeth falling out, and hemorrhages in the tissues of the body. James Cook (1728-1779) provided his crews with sauerkraut, salted cabbage, and a concoction called "marmalade of Carrots," which, inadvertently or not, staved off scurvy. In 1795, after a British naval surgeon observed that citrus prevented the disease, the regulated administration of lime juice began in the British navy.

In the early 1900s two Norwegian doctors, Axel Holst and Theodor Frolich, discovered that withholding fresh food from guinea pigs brought on the symptoms of scurvy. Still, the prevailing thought in Shackleton's time was that scurvy was caused by a kind of food poisoning that could be staved off by

This print depicts Royal Navy surgeon James Lind giving citrus fruits to sailors. Lind, who was Scottish, is credited with introducing citrus to the Royal Navy as a way of preventing scurvy—hence the term "limey" to describe British sailors.

sterilizing—boiling the food in water or whatever. Yet explorers in the Arctic should have figured out that the Eskimos' apparent immunity to the disease was because the only edible food in their harsh environment was what they could fetch from the sea—fish, seal, and whale meat, which are rich in the proper nutrients.

On the explorers' sledging diet of pemmican, oatmeal, and biscuits, the first signs of scurvy appeared in about three months. One more month and physical strength began to flag, the legs stiff and painful, with dark patches from the thighs to the ankles. After five or six months, the condition became truly desperate and led to painful death.

in such bad shape that when they finally arrived back at the Hut after three months on the Barrier, Scott sent him home, to Shackleton's despair, on the relief ship *Morning*.

The *Morning* had arrived in McMurdo Sound to return the entire expedition, but the *Discovery* had frozen in. Scott refused to return—deciding instead to winter over on *Discovery* and try for the pole again next season. When word of this decision got back to the Admiralty in London, it did not reflect well on Scott. A second try for the pole would be expensive; the expedition was out of money. Since it was now too late to rescue Scott before the onset of the Antarctic winter, the new plan was to retrieve him as soon as the ice broke up the following spring. When Shackleton arrived in London, he was told that *Morning* was being sent back again to get Scott—and to make sure Scott complied, the navy was sending along a second relief ship, a sturdy whaler named *Terra Nova*. Shackleton was offered command of the *Terra Nova*—an opportune assignment after his ignominious return, as it would put him in the position of rescuing Scott, whom he had come to think of as a rival. But he declined. For one thing, Shackleton had decided to marry Emily, and their romance took precedence over polar exploration.

That would not be the case for long, however. On the voyage home from Antarctica, Shackleton had already begun formulating plans for his own attempt at the pole. Going back to rescue Scott would delay those efforts. This, as much as his intention toward Emily, influenced his decision to stay put in London.

Discovery* and *Morning

The *Discovery* and its relief ship sit at anchor in McMurdo Sound during the National Antarctic Expedition. After their trek Furthest South, Scott sent the ailing Shackleton home on *Morning*.

The *Nimrod* Sails
1904–1909

JOURNAL ENTRY, 2002 • *Aboard the* Explorer*: The Scotia Sea*

Traveling southeast from the Falklands, the first sight of
land, before South Georgia itself, is a tall sextet of rocks
that rise abruptly from an empty sea, slightly slanted, so
that when I came out on deck, the apparition a half mile off the
bow, I was taken aback by the sight. Marked on the charts as Shag
Rocks, they rise up four or five hundred feet, like the chimney
rocks of the American West, from 9,600 feet down . . . the last
visible sight of the Andes mountain range that like a scorpion's
tail curls out east from Tierra del Fuego far into the South
Atlantic. The day is remarkably beautiful, cloudless, a faint near-
perfect half-moon off to the west, a gibbous moon. The ship is
surrounded by seabirds—the black-browed albatross, skuas,
prions, skittering and ducking into the wave troughs, the
chocolate-hued giant petrel whose color seems almost startling
amongst the inevitable black and white of subantarctic birds.

Shag is another name for cormorant. The droppings from
many thousands of generations have stained the towering rocks a
ghostly white. I wondered idly how many ships in the sailing
days, lost in the mists, have smacked up against these pale rocks;
perhaps they were warned off by the increased volume of the thin
mewing sound that the shags make. About two thousand of
them inhabit the place. With my shipmates I watched them circle
their home, halo-like, from a distance, like bees around a hive. Yet
for all the activity, it is surely one of the loneliest places on earth,

forbidding, utterly inaccessible. The waves crack against the cliffs, the thick spray tumbling up into caverns carved out over the years. I wondered if the rocks were on Shackleton's charts.

Off in the distance someone spotted the first iceberg. At first glance it could have been mistaken for a patch of cloud far on the horizon, but the fading sunlight caught it as if in a beam, and it shone briefly, unmistakably. Up on the foredeck the person who'd first seen it was slapped on the back, a bottle of champagne awarded that night. It was the first iceberg I'd ever seen—and my first reaction was somewhat muted. I associated it with danger, what sank the *Titanic* and so forth . . . quite different from the excitement it generated in others aboard the *Explorer*. Of course, if I'd been the first to spot the iceberg and they'd told me about the champagne that night

We passed the Antarctic Convergence, which is a kind of watery barrier encircling the Antarctic continent where the cold polar surface slides beneath the warmer water from the north. About twenty miles in width, there is no visual evidence of it, though the water temperature as we moved through the seas slowly dropped to a few degrees above zero.

South of the Convergence there are only 39 species of nesting birds— seven penguins, six albatross, eighteen petrels, two skuas, one cormorant, one gull, one tern, one sheathbill, one pintail duck (not the carnivorous), and a pipit—a paucity belied by the enormous numbers of some of the species. Wilson's petrel, a tiny bird (we see a raft of about forty sitting on the surface), is supposedly the most abundant bird in the world.

It reminds me that the Ross Sea side of the continent, where all the early explorations started from, is often referred to as the "Far Side" because there is so little to see. During a two-day crossing on a Russian icebreaker to reach the emperor penguin colonies (admittedly one of the great sights for bird-watchers), a friend of mine, Victor Emanuel, had only seen two birds, a skua and a snowy petrel. His melancholy at the paucity of bird life on the Ross Sea was such that he went below decks to his cabin and began making up a list of the birds he was likely to see from the porch of his cabin home on Galveston Bay in Texas—his intent being that the following year on that exact date he would check from his porch the accuracy of his estimate. What a lovely game of polar solitaire for the destitute birder.

✧ ✧ ✧

Strange indeed that Shackleton, having gone

Ice Island

The nine-to-one ratio of ice under water to ice above water means that a majestic iceberg, like the one below, can measure almost a third of a mile from its highest point to its bottom. Seawater full of microscopic life forms freezes to the underwater base of the iceberg, staining it with different colors. On occasion the iceberg overturns with a surface now of green, black, even stripes.

through such a wrenching
experience with Scott—discovering
that physically he was deficient in
the Antarctic environment, coming
out of it coughing blood—would
ever think of going back into such a
place as the Ross Ice Shelf. What
must have helped enforce his resolve
to return was the huge reception he
received in London. He was lionized
while Scott was still in the
Antarctic...
a situation, in fact, that further
alienated the two since Scott felt
Shackleton was taking too much
credit for Furthest South. But
mainly the lure of the Antarctic was
something else—a mystic pull,
almost a gravitational force that was
irresistible.

Antarctic Map Maker
French explorer Jean-Baptiste
Charcot (in a photo taken around
1900) conducted extensive
charting expeditions around
Antarctica. His coastal maps were
instrumental to later explorers
seeking the Pole.

I came across a number of explanations in my reading. One of the best
were the words of the French explorer Jean Charcot of the ship *Français*:
"What is the secret of that strange and powerful attraction which the polar
regions exercise on all who have once been there? An attraction that is so
strong that no sooner are you back to civilization than you immediately
forget the moral and physical sufferings you have undergone and think
nothing of returning to them again? In what lies the indisputable charm of a
landscape which is both barren and intimidating. Is it the attraction of the
unknown, the elation of struggling to get there, and struggling to live once
you have got there. Is it the pride of achievement, or the pleasure of attempting
something no one has done before, or perhaps the satisfaction of being far
away from all pettiness and meanness? A little of all these things, perhaps, but
I have realized for a long time that in such desolation and bareness I feel the
joy of life more deeply than I do elsewhere..."

Then, of course, there was the lure not only of the Antarctic but of the
Pole itself. Joseph Banks, the botanist on James Cook's first voyage back in the
1770s, wrote, "O, how glorious would it be to set my heel upon the Pole and
turn myself 360 degrees in a second."

Even one of my contemporaries, Thomas Pynchon, writes of the
phenomenon. The protagonist in his novel *V* proclaims, "But I had to reach
it. I had begun to think that there, at one of the only two motionless places
on this gyrating world, I might have peace. I wanted to start at the dead
center of the carousel, if only for a moment, try to catch my bearings..."

Shackleton himself refers to an early, almost empathetic dream in which,
as he wrote, "I seemed to vow to myself that some day I would go to the

FREDERICK COOK: DOCTOR, EXPLORER, LIAR?

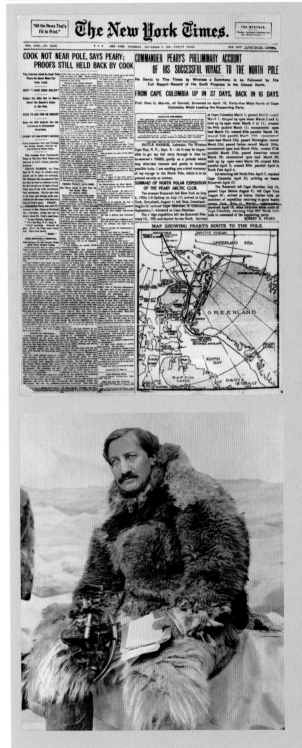

B eing imprisoned in the ice was nothing new in polar exploration. In 1898, Adrien de Gerlache's *Belgica* began drifting in the Bellinghausen Sea. Aboard was the second mate, Roald Amundsen, and a doctor named Frederick Cook. He practiced medicine in Brooklyn—time for very few patients, I would have guessed, because he was also an anthropologist, oceanographer, and explorer. During their thirteen months trapped on the ice, Cook and Amundsen became convinced of how necessary dogs would be to polar travel. During that time, Cook made clothing from penguin skins, and taught languages and literature to the crew. He even theorized how penguin skins attached to the hull could act as buffers against icebergs, their oil helping *Belgica* slither through the ice to the open leads.

But most important of all, Cook urged de Gerlache to get his men to eat fresh meat to stave off scurvy, the first symptoms of which he recognized as a kind of "polar anemia." Fortunately, a steady diet of fresh meat was available everywhere around them—seals, penguins, even the occasional gull-like skua. It was not easy to persuade the men to eat such stuff. Among some sailors it was the belief that the souls of dead seamen lived in penguins. Cook wrote of such meals: "If it is possible to imagine a piece of beef, odifereous [sic] cod fish, and a canvasback duck all roasted in a pot with blood and cod-liver oil for sauce, the illustration will be complete."

Cook also organized betting games and mock beauty contests to get the crew's minds off their predicament. Amundsen wrote of Cook: "He of all this ship's company, was the one man of unfaltering courage, unfailing hope, endless cheerfulness, and unwearied kindness. When anyone was sick, he was at his bedside to comfort him; when anyone was disheartened, he was there to encourage and inspire. And not only was his faith undaunted, but his ingenuity and enterprise were boundless."

Polar exploration was headline news in the early 20th century. When Cook (left) claimed he beat Peary to the North Pole, the controversy dominated newspapers—including the entire front page of the *New York Times*.

Cook was also a liar of considerable note. He later claimed to have climbed Mount McKinley in 1906 with one Ed Barrill, who later recanted and said they hadn't. Cook claimed to have reached the North Pole on his eighth trip into those regions (on April 21, 1908) but was eventually discredited in the Peary-Cook controversy when two Inuits changed their stories and said they knew that he hadn't. Robert Peary, the other claimant to the North Pole, knew Cook from one of his earlier expeditions to Greenland. At the time he praised Cook for his "unruffled patience and coolness in an emergency," but then became an archenemy.

They'd rather be sledging: Looking more like penguins than explorers, (from left to right) Shackleton, Peary, and Amundsen pose in formal wear, nowhere near either Pole. Amundsen's sheer socks and patent leather loafers seem particularly out of character.

Cook's story didn't end with his mendacious polar exploits. His claim and reputation were hardly helped when later he was found guilty of selling fraudulent oil stocks and sent to the federal penitentiary at Leavenworth for fourteen years. He was a model prisoner who worked on a cure for baldness, and taught embroidery to his fellow prisoners. Amundsen regularly went to see him.

Icebound

Explorer James Ross swore off the Antarctic after his ships *Erebus* and *Terror* (above, in an 1842 print) spent months stuck in the ice pack.

region of ice and snow and go on and on till I came to one of the poles of the earth, the end of the axis upon which this great round ball turns."

The only explorer who seems to have said to himself, "That's enough" was Sir James Ross. He came home in the fall of 1843 with *Terror* and *Erebus* after four years and five months at sea, one of the longest expeditions in history. He won all the appropriate awards, received a knighthood, and eventually a peerage. It is recorded that he took only one short boat trip after that—a ferry boat. He'd had enough of it, apparently. He was twelve when he went to sea. He became known as the handsomest man in the Royal Navy, to which a number of splendid portraits of him attest, an attribute, however, that is not of much use in the Antarctic.

Emily's father having died in 1901, Ernest and Emily were free to marry, which they finally did on April 9, at Christchurch Westminster. Settling in to married life, trying to make a name for himself, he dabbled in finance and business, and thought about a career in journalism, having edited a shipboard magazine on the *Discovery* called *The South Polar Times* illustrated by his friend Bill Wilson.

Mainly he enjoyed lecturing about the *Discovery* expedition, and he must have been very good at it. Here is a description by

LEADING MAN

Ross (left) was an early incarnation of the handsome, heroic explorer.

one F. W. Everett, the editor of the *Royal Magazine*. "He had the true sailor's love for spinning a yarn, and many are the work hours I wasted with the best will in the world listening to his stirring adventure in all quarters of the earth … his face, heavy and stern in repose, all alive and lit up with the excitement of retelling his hairbreadth escapes by field and flood. [His] deep, husky voice, rising and falling with the movement of his story [was] sometimes raised, by way of illustrating his point, to a rafter shaking roar … Whether it was the … compelling gesture or the Irishman's natural gift for expression, he made us see the things he spoke of, and held us all spell-bound."

Everett was so taken by Shackleton's skill as a story-teller that he hired him as a subeditor at the *Royal Magazine*. Everett started him out at the lowest level, writing jokes for the back page (an example: "Of the heroine in one of the latest sensational novels it is said: 'Her eye chained him to the spot.' She must have been links-eyed").

Struggling daily with this sort of thing, Shackleton must have quickly realized that the road to the top in journalism was long and arduous, too much so for one as eager for fame and fortune, and after a few months he resigned. Everett must have been sorry to see him go. He wrote of him that whatever he tried next he would be a success at it and that whoever took him ("a stockbroker, a butcher, a carpenter, a theatrical manager") on would not regret it.

His next employer might have taken issue with Everett's assessment. The intercession of his friend Hugh Mill got Shackleton the job of secretary of the Royal Scottish Geographic Society in Edinburgh. He had few qualifications to run an academic institution, but with his charm and his outgoing manner, he made quite an impact on an institution where in rather drab surroundings employees in the dark suits of that era worked in the kind of silence broken only by the slow pendulum click of a grandfather clock. Shackleton burst in on this wearing tweed jackets and lounged about smoking cigarettes. He introduced a typewriter in an office that had seen only quill pens. And a telephone. He wrote to Mill, "a telephone! You should have seen the faces of some of the old chaps when it started to ring today."

Emily came up from London and they settled in to married life on the outskirts of Edinburgh. They lived comfortably. Shackleton joined a golf club and the two played the course together, Emily turning out to be the better player. Perhaps that riled him, being as competitive as he was. On one occasion in

Dashing Hero
This rather stylized portrait of Shackleton was probably shot in a London studio. Posed photos of explorers simulating their adventures were quite common, and suited Shackleton's flair for publicity.

FRANK SHACKLETON

Frank Shackleton enjoyed easy access to Dublin Castle (above), when the Irish crown jewels were stolen from the tower.

Ernest Shackleton's brother Frank turned out to be quite a problem. His career had started off innocently enough—an interest in gardening that led to a rose-growing concern which provided an entrée to high society. Two years younger than Ernest, he resembled a thinner version, but dressed in such stylish clothes that he was considered something of a fop, a description somewhat reinforced by the company he kept—the homosexual set who clustered around the court of King Edward VII. In Dublin Frank lived with Sir Arthur Vicars, the crown's representative in Ireland who held court in a tower in Dublin Castle. He also kept a luxurious flat in London's Park Lane without the apparent means to support such a lifestyle. Because of his connections in the banking world, Frank helped his brother raise credit for his expedition to the south on *Nimrod.* But before long, he got involved in shady deals that made him a liability. Just as *Nimrod* was preparing to sail in the summer of 1907, the Irish crown jewels were stolen from a safe in the tower in Dublin Castle where Sir Arthur Vicars entertained. An inside job was assumed. Frank was the chief suspect (he subsequently bought a town house in London and a very expensive car, again without any visible source of income), but was exonerated, possibly for political reasons, for fear of a scandal that would have exposed a number of homosexuals in the Royal Court.

The case was never solved, the jewels never recovered. In 1913, Frank was charged with defrauding an elderly woman whose money he was managing, and spent nearly a year in prison. Upon his release he changed his last name to Mellor.

Shackleton disowned him after the return of the *Endurance* expedition in 1916, and Frank ended his days living quietly as an antiques dealer, specializing (as one might suspect) in precious stones.

the offices of the Scottish Geographic Society he caught one of his assistants driving a golf ball into a heavy curtain at the far end of a room. Rather than reprimanding him, Shackleton took the club and began hitting practice shots himself, finally hitting a ball through a crack in the curtain, so the story goes, out a window pane and onto the street.

His official duties at the Society bored Shackleton, and he spent a considerable amount of time in London trying to set up financial ventures and get-rich-quick schemes, many of them with his brother Frank, all of which came to naught. In January 1905, Ernest quit the post at the Royal Scottish Geographic Society to try politics.

Through contacts he'd made at the Geographic Society, Shackleton managed to get on the Conservative Party ticket for Parliament, representing Edinburgh. Although his fervent speeches (mostly on the subject of protecting British trade from German encroachment) were admired, he lost the January 1905 election as the Liberals (including a young Winston Churchill) swept into office across the country.

Shackleton next took a job at the Parkhead Engineering Works, a shipbuilding concern in Glasgow. The job description was vague—a greeter of sorts, charged with charming and entertaining clients who visited the shipyard. But once again it put him close to powerful people who could be of financial assistance for his intended expedition south, in particular William Beardmore, whom he had met during his turbulent times with the Geographic Society.

Meanwhile, Scott had returned from the Antarctic, and in his lectures and journals—which were published as *The Voyage of the Discovery*—he was telling a very different story than Shackleton's. Most damaging was Scott's assertion that Shackleton's illness pretty much prevented their reaching the pole. Shackleton was outraged. It compelled him to move forward with his own expedition as quickly as possible, in hopes of beating Scott to the Pole.

Unlike Scott, whose government-sponsored expeditions held at least a veneer of scientific inquiry, Shackleton decided to dispense with the high-minded rhetoric about collecting rocks and ice crystals, and reach the pole for the greater glory of England. The expedition, he told potential backers like Beardmore, would in fact be profitable. Speeches and even a film of the journey would generate an income for his sponsors.

In February of 1907, attracted by the possibilities of financial return, Beardmore signed on

Rarefied Company

Fame found Shackleton in the company of wealthy and influential Britishers, among them tea magnate Sir Thomas Lipton (below right). He spent less time at home with Emily, and more time with his friends at London clubs.

for £7,000—about half the money needed. A few months later, Shackleton got £8,000 from a series of investors, including Edward Guinness of the brewing family.

With the money, Shackleton was able to secure a 300-ton, 41-year-old Newfoundland sealer called *Nimrod*, named after the biblical hunter in Genesis. He had wanted a larger, better-appointed ship, but finances dictated he accept this small workhorse, which cost just £5,000. She had sails and an auxiliary steam engine, with a top speed of about six knots.

Shackleton had hoped to persuade many of the crewmen with whom he had sailed on *Discovery* to join him—but they declined, either from loyalty to Scott, previous engagements, or just plain dread of another Antarctic journey. The most notable refusal came from Edward (Bill) Wilson, his friend from *Discovery*. Shackleton had written him him "I want the job done and you are the best man in the world for it...Come, Billy...Don't say No till we have a talk. Don't say No at all."

Wilson wrote back that he was unavailable because he was deep in his scientific work at the time. A disease had infected the grouse population and on behalf of Lord Lovat, he was trying to save the bird for the English gentry to gun down. During the course of writing the *Grouse Report* he was to dissect over two thousand grouse before discovering that minute tract worms were the source of the disease. Shackleton wrote again, pleading "England before grouse!", but to no avail.

One of the reasons Wilson may have been reluctant to join the *Nimrod* expedition was that Shackleton had planned an additional, indeed lunatic,

The *Nimrod* Sails
Thirty thousand spectators showed up to see *Nimrod* off from Lyttelton, New Zealand. So little bunker space was available for coal that she had to be towed to the ice by a tramp steamer, the *Koonya*. The living quarters on board were hardly suitable—fourteen of the crew in a space, one of them said later, "not fit for 10 dogs."

element. He would not only reach the South Pole but drag with him a portable boat he'd named *Raymond,* after his infant son. Then his idea was to continue on past the pole with the boat and launch it into the Weddell Sea and sail north for a rendezvous with *Nimrod.*

Fortunately, the *Raymond* never arrived at dockside, much to Shackleton's chagrin, and *Nimrod* sailed without her on July 30, 1907. Six months later she arrived in McMurdo Sound.

✧ ✧ ✧

JOURNAL ENTRY, 2002 • *Aboard the* Explorer: *The Scotia Sea*

At dinner I sat with one of the passengers, Bob Baines, who had joined the ship in the Falklands. His original plan had been to get to the South Pole. The British supply Antarctic bases from the Falklands and he had an idea he could hitch a ride to the South Pole on one of their planes. He had been ill-informed. No such schedule. It was a shame because the South Pole was on his list of goals. The Falklands were also on his list. "Why the Falklands?" I asked. Well, the year before he had seen a pseudodocumentary by an Argentine director at the Sundance Film Festival about an Argentine who went to the Falklands with the intention of impregnating all the local females so that the future inhabitants would all be Argentine. After seeing the film, he had put the Falklands on his list of goals.

"You want to get to the Falklands to see how susceptible its women might be to this sort of scheme?" I asked.

"Not necessarily, " he said. "But it made the Falklands a point of interest."

He went on to say that he has about three hundred and forty on his list of goals—inspired originally by Joseph Campbell, the historian and mythologist, who promoted the idea of "follow your bliss," and by John Gadded, the explorer who, when he was sixteen, had made such a list of his own—kayaking the length of the Nile, taking off from an aircraft carrier, and so on, as well as more sensitive ones about composing music, conducting scientific studies, including milking a rattlesnake (he got himself bitten). By the time Gadded had reached his late 70s he had done almost all of them, including surviving the rattlesnake bite.

"I became friends with John and his wife Carol. My wife Christine and I traveled with them to the Amazon and the Galapagos a few years back."

"So now you can cross the Falklands off your life list."

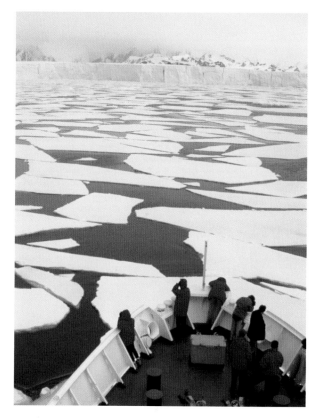

The Frozen Sea
As the *Explorer* gets underway, ice creates a jagged, frozen quilt across the Scotia Sea.

"Right."

He asked if I had such a list.

I said that I was always on the lookout for rare birds.

"There's a duck, a carnivorous duck. Perhaps in South Georgia."

"An excellent goal."

"And the South Georgia pipit. The duck wasn't in the Falklands," I said. "The carnivorous part is probably exaggerated."

Bob shrugged. "You were following your bliss," he said.

✧　✧　✧

Scott had been furious when he heard about Shackleton's *Nimrod* expedition. He had written him that he also intended to return to the South and therefore Shackleton had no right to use the facilities and routes that he had established during the *Discovery* expedition.

It became a public matter, and Shackleton was forced into a promise that he would not approach the pole from anywhere in McMurdo Sound, nor use *Discovery*'s winter quarters on Ross Island in the sound. It was in a sense a gentleman's agreement (Antarctica belonged to no country, much less any single man), but it carried the force of honor and had been respected by others. The French explorer Charcot deliberately avoided the Ross Sea area, appreciating it as Scott's turf, and in doing so earned Scott's approval of being "the gentleman of the Pole."

When *Nimrod* reached the Ross Sea, Shackleton broke the promise, although he had an excuse: The inlet where he had intended to set up his winter quarters had calved off the glacier. So with great reluctance (he was a Freemason and Freemasonry makes a particular point of being true to one's word), he decided to use Ross Island as his base and built his hut on Cape Royds. Scott subsequently heard about this when the *Nimrod*, having left off Shackleton and his men, arrived in New Zealand. He denounced Shackleton as a "liar." It was an act of betrayal that apparently haunted Shackleton to the end of his days.

✧　✧　✧

JOURNAL ENTRY, 2002 • *Aboard the* Explorer: *The Scotia Sea*

I never thought I'd hear anything in real life aboard *Explorer* to match the ill-preparedness of those early polar expeditions. But then last night I was sitting around at the bar with four young Englishmen. They appeared after just about everyone had gone below to their cabins—the tendency is to go to bed not long after dinner. They were hitchhiking on the *Explorer* (we picked them up in the Falkland Islands) on the way to South Georgia. They told me they had signed up with a demolition team sent to complete the destruction of whaling station buildings on South Georgia that had been deserted for years and were falling apart. One of them with a wide grin admitted that he had

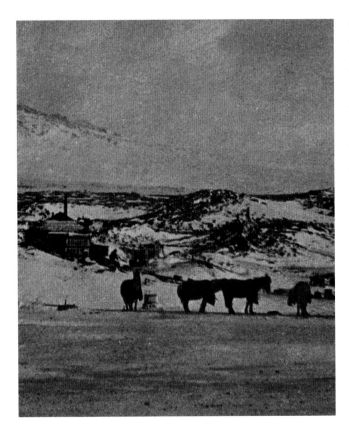

Bad Idea

Ponies turned out to be a poor choice of draft animal for Antarctica. Their diet of grain meant their food had to be hauled in, whereas dogs could eat penguins and seals.

signed up thinking he was on his way to a village its inhabitants saw fit to call South Pole—a small community in County Devon! I shook my head in disbelief. The others nodded. Apparently there *is* such a place. He'd signed up and here he was on his way to a ghost community on an island thousands of miles away from where he *thought* he was going. One had to hope he had sufficient clothes in his pack!

✧ ✧ ✧

After spending the bitter Antarctic winter on Ross Island, Shackleton left for the South Pole on October 29, 1908—six years after the *Discovery* trip—with one motor car and four ponies from Manchuria and Siberia. The car went a few miles and then got stuck. The ponies were the idea of a big-game hunter named Frederick Jackson, who had spent some time training horses at high latitudes. He convinced Shackleton to try them despite all the practical problems, such as providing bales of hay to feed the animals (dogs, of course, could eat off the land—seal, penguin).

Like Scott, Shackleton was averse to using dogs. In his book *The South Pole*, Roald Amundsen wrote "The great difference between Scott's expedition and ours lay in the choice of draught animals. Scott had come to the conclusion that Manchurian ponies and motor sledges would be superior to dogs as a means on transport... there must, I told myself, be a basic misunderstanding in the British attitude. Perhaps the dog didn't comprehend its master—or was it that the master didn't comprehend the dog."

Shackleton had three men with him: Lieutenant Jameson Boyd Adams, the second in command on *Nimrod*, like Shackleton a former master in the merchant service; Eric Marshall, the chief surgeon, a Cambridge graduate who had met Shackleton at a house party and impulsively, under the spell of the explorer's rhetoric, had agreed to join the expedition; and Frank Wild, later to serve as second-in-command on the *Endurance*.

It is easy to chart how Shackleton fared by following the fortunes of the four ponies. One of them kicked Adams before they got underway, but it was their last mutinous gesture. A month and a half out, the first, Chinaman by name, became so weakened that on November 21 on the 81st parallel, quite close to Scott's Furthest South, he was put down with a pistol shot and his

CLIMBING MOUNT EREBUS

Six men from the *Nimrod* expedition were the first to climb Mount Erebus. At 13,500 feet, Erebus is one of the twenty largest volcanos in the world. It is still active and is in a near-constant state of low-level eruption—huffing and puffing, emitting noxious fumes, and throwing off car-sized boulders. The volcano was first seen by the British explorer Sir James Clark Ross in 1841. His men described rivers of lava flowing down its sides. He named it Erebus after one of his two ships, in mythology the son of Chaos and Darkness. A smaller inactive volcano adjacent is named Terror, after his second ship. Shackleton proposed the climb, though he himself did not go. Eric Marshall, the doctor on board, worried about the state of Shackleton's health, and insisted on examining him before the climb; Shackleton evaded the issue by electing to stay behind.

The group set off, totally ill-equipped for a climb that for a mountaineer is relatively easy. It took them

Smoke rises from the crater of Mount Erebus, one of two active volcanoes in the Antarctic region. (The other is Deception Island.) Attempts have been made to harness its heat for the earth science laboratory at McMurdo Station, with no luck.

five days to reach the crater's edge. They peered down to watch rising puffs of steam and hear distant rumbles from its interior. One member of the team missed the sight: Philip Brocklehurst, suffering altitude sickness and frostbite, had been left two thousand feet below the crater in his sleeping bag. The group had celebrated his twenty-first birthday on the way. Brocklehurst came on *Nimrod* as an assistant geologist, surveyor, and photographer. According to his diaries he admired Shackleton for being "Bohemian," "fond of the ladies," and "extravagant with taxis." He would have gone on with him for the pole if he had not lost a toe to frostbite coming back from the Erebus climb.

POLAR WINTER

Polar winter is the most extreme climate on Earth. Temperatures have been recorded as low as 126 degrees Fahrenheit below zero. The windchill temperatures can drop to minus 166 Fahrenheit. It is said that a fish drawn up through the ice would be so frozen solid within five seconds that it would have to be cut with a saw. At the South Pole, the sun disappears completely for about 70 days, dipping below the horizon on or about March 22, and emerges in full view—in Captain James Cook's memorable description "like a withered orange"—around September 22.

Even modern aircraft and vehicles brave the bitter cold and profound darkness of the Antarctic winter only in emergency situations—as in this photo from April 2001, which depicts a Canadian plane preparing to evacuate an ailing scientist from the South Pole research station.

Thus attempts to reach the Pole were always made in the 24-hour daylight and relative warmth of the austral summer, as high as five degrees Fahrenheit above zero at the Pole, which often necessitated waiting out winter on the ship—warmed by the heat of the coal stove, and illuminated, however dimly, by lantern light.

body prepared for food—no compunctions about eating horse meat. A week later, Grisi was shot, and two days later so was Shackleton's pony, Quan. The pole was still four hundred miles away. That left Socks, Frank Wild's pony. By this time they had long surpassed Scott's Furthest South by two full degrees of latitude. At the end of the ice shelf they had reached the tongue of a vast glacier that Shackleton named the Beardmore Glacier. On the third day on this glacier, Socks—"noble little Socks" in Marshall's affectionate words—fell into a crevasse to his end, "not a sign of him down this terrible abyss & not a sound to be heard."

It is thought that if Socks had survived and struggled on with the men to within one hundred miles of the pole that he would have provided them with enough food to make a final dash. As it was, Shackleton decided to turn back on January 9, 1909, after getting within ninety-seven miles of the pole. "We have shot our bolt," he wrote.

On the return trip, with the men now in the traces pulling the sledges themselves, their health began to deteriorate rapidly, Marshall's in particular. Finally, too weak to continue, he was left in a tent in Adams's care while Shackleton and Wild, dumping most of their gear, made a dash for the base camp to get help—across the Shelf for thirty-six hours without rest, arriving only to find that their base camp was deserted. *Nimrod's* captain, Frederick Pryce Evans, with the rendezvous date long past, had assumed that Shackleton and his group were somewhere entombed in the ice. Worried about the oncoming weather conditions, afraid the ship was in danger of becoming frozen in, he had pulled up anchor and moved out. It was only after a testy argument at sea that he was persuaded to return and leave a wintering search party.

"No happier sight ever met the eyes of man," Wild wrote when *Nimrod's* crow's nest was sighted.

Now it became a matter of returning to fetch Adams and Marshall. Such was Shackleton's sense of responsibility and determination (which would serve him so well later on) that he went back himself to retrieve them. He asked for three volunteers from the ship to go with him. The three men who responded were Douglas Mawson, A. F. Mackay, and a stoker named McGillan. After the forty-eight-hour trip in blizzard conditions there and back, one of them, Mackay, fell into the *Nimrod's* wardroom crying out for the ship's doctor: "Into thy hands, oh doc, I deliver my body and my spirit." He and Mawson spent two days in bed, the athletic stoker for five days. As for Shackleton, he went to the bridge and took *Nimrod* out to sea.

Furthest Foursome

The four men of the Furthest South trek (from left: Wild, Shackleton, Marshall, and Adams) pose on board the *Nimrod* after their harrowing race to safety.

South Georgia
1910–1914

If one couldn't get to a pole, the next best target in world opinion had been to get Furthest South (or North). Fridtjof Nansen made Furthest North (near the 86th parallel) in 1895, widely acclaimed for doing so despite failing in his objective to reach the pole.

Shackleton made the best of his Furthest South. Returning to London a celebrated national hero, he was knighted. He went on the lecture circuit, dictated a book entitled *The Heart of the Antarctic*, and turned the *Nimrod* into a museum to make money to pay his debts. He traveled to the United States, where he was feted in every city he visited, his name in headlines in the local papers. He took in a couple of baseball games. The June 25, 1910, issue of *Sporting Life* reports him as saying, "It is a fine game, and I was strongly impressed by the way the men pulled together... I also noted the generous way the crowd applauded the good fielding of their opponents. I thought that was sportmanslike. The 'game' however, seems a bit too scientific for sport."

Later, in Chicago, Shackleton saw a Cubs game and once again remarked on the fielding—how much better it was compared to cricket. "Over in England and in the colonies we cricketers can bat better than they do here, I believe, but the fielders muff the ball a lot. A catch which seems so easy here brings forth tumults of applause over there."

The writer of the piece editorialized rather grandly: "Taken all together, Sir Ernest considers baseball a wonderful game,

Explorer Envy

This cartoon made fun of the rivalry between polar explorers—and the increasingly hollow claims of Dr. Frederick Cook, whose "proofs" of polar discovery were discredited by the University of Copenhagen. Newspaper cartoons like this reflected the huge public interest in the race to the South Pole.

CHEVY STARTS UP

1911
• In the fall of 1911, Swiss-born mechanic and racecar driver Louis Chevrolet incorporates the Chevrolet Motor Company in Detroit. He plans to manufacture high-performance cars with a new engine that he designed. His partner in the venture is financier William Durant.

worthy of any nation—which may be a splendid tribute, considering that Shackleton, apart from his scientific side, is a thorough, all-round sportsman and a noted cricketer."

But after his Antarctica experience, games of sport—and every other aspect of normal life—rather bored him. He was rarely at home with Emily, preferring to make the rounds of London clubs. In those environs, there was always a chance of finding a patron for what was really on his mind since his return—getting back into Antarctic adventure and reaching the pole.

But the startling news arrived. The pole had been reached on December 14, 1911, not by Scott but by the Norwegian Amundsen. In London, as all across Europe, the news was announced with blaring headlines. The *Daily Mirror* had a photograph on its front page that showed a member of the Norwegian expedition standing at the pole in the snow beside their country's flag.

Amundsen had appeared on the South Pole scene rather unexpectedly. His original project had been to be the first to reach the North Pole. When he heard news of Peary's success, he changed his plans, and decided to try for the South Pole instead. He knew that others—Scott, perhaps the Americans, the Japanese—might hear of this, so he kept the secret to himself, even from his own crew, until they had left Norway. One wonders at the surprise of those aboard, who assumed the expedition was headed north. ("Ahem, we have a slight change of course.") A determined opportunist, Amundsen had a favorite saying: "Success is a woman to be won, not courted. You've got to seize her and carry her off, not stand under her window with a mandolin."

When he arrived in the Antarctic on his ship *Fram*, he set up his base (Framheim) in the Bay of Whales, sixty miles closer to the pole than Scott's encampment on Ross Island. By chance, Scott happened to send a reconnaissance group down the Shelf to the Bay of Whales, where to their surprise and surely to their discomfort they came across Amundsen's *Fram*. The officer from both camps exchanged somewhat stiff greetings. They each invited the other to a dinner on their respective ships; Amundsen grumbled that some of his men caught colds from the visitors. Both parties—Scott's especially—obviously sensed that it was a race for the pole, as if a stranger had suddenly ranged up alongside at a starting line.

Amundsen started for the pole on October 19, 1911, with 52 dogs, four sledges, and four companions, traveling as many as twenty-four miles a day. His timetable was so carefully planned that at one juncture they had time to take a side jaunt and climb a mountain they decided to call Mt. Betty, after Amundsen's childhood nurse.

At the halfway point, as it had been planned, half of their dogs were killed to provide fresh meat to sustain the remaining dogs and men on the push to the pole and back. The night of the killing Amundsen pumped up the Primus stove in his tent in the hopes of deadening the sound of the shots. "It was hard," he wrote, "but it had to be...I am not a nervous man, but at the sound of the first shot I found myself trembling. Shot now followed shot in quick succession, echoing uncannily over the great white plain. Each time a trusty servant lost his life."

He reached the pole on December 14, his men holding back the dogs so their leader would be the first living thing to the estimated site of the pole. There was no cheering. Each of the five held the flagpole as they drove it into the snow.

Amundsen offered a puzzling statement about his moment of triumph: "I have never known any man to be placed in such a diametrically opposite position to the goal of his desires as I was at that moment. The North Pole had attracted me from childhood, and here I was at the South Pole."

After three days verifying their position with navigating instruments, they celebrated their achievement with cigars. They left behind some excess articles for Scott—a reindeer bag full of clothing, including fur mittens, and an

Amundsen at the Pole
When Shackleton heard the news that Amundsen had reached the Pole, he cabled him "Heartiest congratulations magnificent achievement." He subsequently wrote in the *Daily Mail*, "Amundsen is perhaps the greatest Polar explorer of today." Note the magnificent condition of the dogs, which Amundsen used brilliantly.

English-made hypsometer, a meteorological instrument for measuring pressure. It was a parting gift Shackleton had given Amundsen.

A note was left for Scott. "Dear Captain Scott: As you probably are the first to reach this area after us, I will ask you to kindly forward this letter to King Haakon VII. If you can use any of the articles left in the tent please do not hesitate to do so. The sledge left outside may be of use to you. With kind regards I wish you a safe return. Yours truly, Roald Amundsen."

Scott had left for the pole on October 24, just five days later than Amundsen, and was in trouble from the start. The final group—Scott, Oates, Bowers, Evans, and Wilson—were a month behind Amundsen when they finally arrived. It is hard to conceive of their dismay discovering the artifacts of Amundsen's triumph, especially the letter. They wrote about the occasion in their diaries, their reaction by no means the same. Wilson, who had finished his studies on grouse disease and had been persuaded to join the expedition, is almost matter-of-fact. He writes on January 16, 1912: "We got away at 8 A.M. and made 7.5 miles by 1:15. Lunched and then in 5.3 miles came on a black flag and Norwegians' sledge and dog tracks running about N.E. and S.W. We camped here and examined the tracks and discussed things."

There is more but it is all technical. The next day, January 17, Wilson writes, "it was a very bitter day," but he is talking about the weather (22 below zero Fahrenheit), not the disappointment of being second to the Pole. The only reference to the pole is the line, "He [Amundsen] has beaten us in so far as he has made a race of it."

Scott was far more emotional. "The worst has happened—All the day dreams must go and terrible enough for us to have laboured to it without the reward of priority." The next day he wrote, "Great God! This is an awful place. Now for the run home and a desperate struggle. I wonder if we can do it."

One of the reasons for their subsequent tragedy was that Scott never lost sight of the fact that theirs was also a scientific exploration. The sledges beside the collapsed tent in which the three frozen bodies were later found held fossil rocks they had picked up on the top of the Beardmore Glacier—the fossils from trees that grew at the edge of some inland sea 2.5 to 3.2 million years ago. Scott had written in his diary, "…Wilson, with his sharp eyes, has picked several plant

AMUNDSEN'S END

He said "Shackleton's name will for evermore be engraved with letters of fire in the history of the Antarctic Exploration."

A little over two decades after discovering the Pole (in 1926), Amundsen may have been the first to cross the North Pole by air—from the Norwegian island of Spitsbergen to Alaska, in the dirigible *Norge*, with the Italian explorer Umberto Nobile. (American Admiral Richard Byrd had claimed the same feat earlier, although his account is now disputed.) In 1928, when Nobile's dirigible *Italia* was wrecked on its return from the North Pole, Amundsen, though he had quarreled bitterly with Nobile over who should be credited for their flight with the *Norge*, went to the Arctic looking for him; his plane went down in the sea; apart from some wreckage that later washed ashore, no trace of Amundsen was ever found.

impressions, the last a piece of coal with beautifully traced leaves in layers, and some excellently preserved impressions of thick stems, showing cellular structure."

So they tallied when they should have been hastening north for McMurdo Sound.

It was almost as if the realization of being second to the pole would be mitigated by some earthshaking scientific study. Indeed, the insistence on scientific exploration, especially on Wilson's part (on occasion he said the pole was of no interest to him) could well have sealed their doom. Wilson, in his last letter, ever the scientist, regretted that he would not live to see the publication of his work on the grouse disease. Earlier he had written a letter to a friend in which he said, "I shall be frightfully keen to see if the mail brings me a copy of the *Grouse Report*."

Their last encampment was only eighteen miles from a depot of food and fuel.

The news of Scott's death reached Britain in February 1913, almost a year after it had happened, and it caused a great tumult of national mourning—especially after his diaries, edited heavily by J. M. Barrie, the author of *Peter Pan*, were published. His final message, discovered in the wind-blown tent, was surely repeated from every stage and pulpit, and memorized by every schoolboy, epitomizing as it did the post-Victorian élan of the period: "We shall die like gentlemen. I think this will show that the Spirit of pluck and power to endure has not passed out of our race ... Had we lived, I should have had a tale to tell of hardihood, endurance, and courage of my companions, which would have stirred the heart of every Englishman. These rough notes and our dead bodies must tell the tale."

The last entry in his diary, March 29, 1912, reads, "It seems a pity, but I do not think I can write more."

✧　　✧　　✧

JOURNAL ENTRY, 2002 • *Aboard the* Explorer: *The Scotia Sea*
I went aft to watch the black-browed albatross, glider-like, with wings that are stiff and fixed to their bodies but which somehow feel the air drafts and flurries rising off the tumult of the ocean below so that they can tilt and turn without ever a wingbeat. It is if they are glider-kites attached by an invisible wire to the stern and kept aloft by the wind of our passage through the seas.

> we shall stick it out to the end but we are getting weaker of course and the end cannot be far. It seems a pity but I do not think I can write more —
> R. Scott
> Last Entry —
> For Gods Sake look after our people

Scott's Farewell
The doomed men wrote goodbye letters to wives, parents, and friends. Scott left a "Message to the Public"—a detailed, if somewhat rambling account of what had happened. It included an appeal for assistance to the dying explorers' families: 'Surely a great rich country like ours will see that those who are dependent on us are properly provided for ... For God's sake look after our people'.

With them in sight are smaller ocean birds—prions, Wilson's storm petrels, shearwaters (aptly named because they seem to do exactly that through the thin wave-crests), but the albatrosses (I'd never seen one before) I watched until the cold set in and I hauled open the big steel safety door and stepped into the warmth of the ship.

I went below to my cabin and read the wonderful section in *Moby Dick* about the albatross that falls on the deck of *Pequod*, indeed Ishmael's first albatross!

I remember the first albatross I saw. It was during a gale in waters hard upon the Antarctic seas. From my forenoon watch below, I ascended to the overcrowded deck; and there, dashed upon the main hatch, I saw a regal, feathery thing of unspotted whiteness, and with a hooked, Roman bill sublime. At intervals, it arched forth its vast archangel wings, as if to embrace some holy ark. Wondrous flutterings and throbbings shook it. Though bodily unharmed, it uttered strange cries, as some king's ghost in supernatural distress. Through its inexpressible, strange eyes, methought I peeped to secrets which took hold of God. An Abraham before the angels, I bowed myself; the white thing was so white, its wings so wide, and in those forever exiled waters, I had lost the miserable warping memories of tradition and of towns. Long I gazed at that prodigy of plumage. I cannot tell, can only hint, at things that darted through me then.

✧　　✧　　✧

However Shackleton felt about the death of Scott, he stayed busy raising money for his next venture: what he called rather grandiosely "The Imperial Trans-Antarctic Expedition"… to cross the continent from one side to the other.

There is a note of desperation to Shackleton's new idea. Most sensible people, once the pole was discovered, would have thrown in the towel—game over—especially as his rival Scott was now dead. But Shackleton was ever restless. His life at sea had ill-prepared him for quiet domestic life, and his time at the Royal Scottish Geographic Society had shown how impossible it was for him to sit in an office all day.

Apparently many of Shackleton's backers on the *Nimrod* expedition sensed this as a lost cause, and bowed out. Sir Clements Markham of London's Royal Geographical Society, of which Shackleton was a fellow, seemed equally skeptical. He wrote to the organization's secretary that Shackleton's new plan appeared to be designed "solely for self-advertisement."

There were other factors beyond Shackleton's control. Increasing tension with Germany dominated national

Icy Grave

The search party built this cairn of snow above the bodies (and collapsed tent) of Scott, Wilson and Bowers. The cross is made of skis lashed together.

Big Bird

The wandering albatross is the largest of all the seabirds, with a wing span of more than 11 feet. Satellite tracking tells us that these birds cover the Southern oceans for thousands of miles on a single foraging trip. The birds I was watching could very well have circumnavigated the planet.

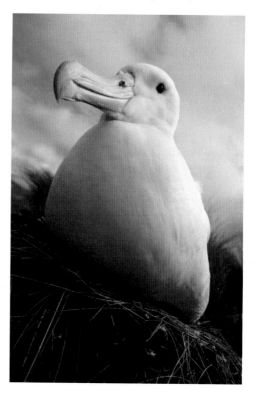

PRICELESS BISCUIT

Besides being rather stale by now, this *Nimrod* biscuit would be an expensive snack.

Frank Wild, who had been with Shackleton on the *Nimrod* expedition, had not thought much of him at the start, but then came to realize that Shackleton had that one indispensable quality of leadership—putting his men first. There had been a vivid example: on the return trip, desperately weakened by hunger, Shackleton gave up his own breakfast biscuit of the four rationed and insisted that Wild have it. Wild was so impressed that he wrote, "I do not suppose that anyone else in the world can thoroughly know much generosity and sympathy was shown by this; I DO by GOD I shall never forget it. Thousands of pounds would not have bought that one biscuit."

He was close. A recent Christie's catalogue featured an auction of artifacts from polar expeditions. Taking up an entire page was a color photograph of a Huntley & Palmer's biscuit from the *Nimrod* expedition. The expected price for that single biscuit was listed as between $1,600 and $2,300, but it didn't sell.

debate. The sinking of the *Titanic* in April 1912 after striking an iceberg cast a pall over polar sea adventures. Indeed, Shackleton himself was called upon to testify in the official inquiry. Winston Churchill, then first lord of the Admiralty, wrote in an Admiralty minute that "enough life and money has been spent on this sterile quest…the Pole has already been discovered. What is the use of another expedition?"

But as always, Shackleton turned on his charm. In a prospectus he referred to it as "the last great Polar journey that can be made. It will be a greater journey than the journey to the Pole and back."

He convinced David Lloyd George, then chancellor of the Exchequer, to pledge £10,000 of government support. He won the good graces of the War Office. Even the Royal Geographical Society helped. He got Churchill to allow navy shipmates who had accompanied Scott to go along on the new expedition.

Backers came forward. Guinness (one of the few from *Nimrod* who remained faithful) were promised a cut of future earnings from film rights. A London newspaper, *The Daily Chronicle*, bought the rights both to the expedition's story and photographs. Then three last-minute contributions came in—first from a Birmingham magnate named Dudley Docker (who gave £10,000), then from Janet Stancomb-Wills, a philanthropist who was somehow inveigled into a major but secret contribution, and finally from a Scottish tycoon, James Caird, who had made his fortune in the jute trade. Caird had such generous notions about philanthropy that he asked for nothing in return. His no-strings-attached contribution of £24,000 assured that the expedition would go forward.

Shackleton's plan called for navigating a ship through the pack ice of the Weddell Sea (the southernmost reach of the Atlantic Ocean), landing a party on the Filchner Ice Shelf, then trekking across uncharted mountain and glacier-strewn land to the South Pole, crossing over it and down to the Beardmore Glacier, then to McMurdo Sound in the Ross Sea— a distance of almost 2,000 miles…more or less like sledging from Chicago to Los Angeles during an ice age. On the other side of the continent, on McMurdo Sound, a second ship would be waiting for him.

Landing parties from this ship were to lay down food depots every degree of latitude (every 60 miles) on the Ross Ice Shelf up to the foot of the Beardmore Glacier so that Shackleton and his group could sustain themselves on the second half of their trek.

For his lead ship, Shackleton bought a newly built Norwegian barquentine—three masts, only the foremost of which was square-rigged. Oddly enough, it had been built to take tourists into the polar regions, with a fully equipped darkroom for those with cameras. The idea was ahead of its time, and the plan fell through. But the ship, named *Polaris*, was perfect for Shackleton. He paid £11,600 and renamed her *Endurance* after his family motto: *Fortitudine Vincimus*—"By Endurance We Conquer."

The second ship, *Aurora*, another Newfoundland sealer like *Nimrod*, was already in the South Pacific and thus perfectly positioned to go south. He bought her for £3,200.

The *Endurance* left London on August 1, 1914—just as World War I was breaking out. Shackleton was stunned and saddened, assuming that his expedition would be called off. Indeed, he offered the ship to the government, which declined. The First Lord of the Admiralty, Churchill, cabled "Proceed."

The *Endurance* Sails
Shackleton is presented with a bough of heather as the Endurance prepares to set sail from London in August 1914. To the left, in derby hat, is the expedition's artist, George Marston.

✧ ✧ ✧

JOURNAL ENTRY, 2002 • *Salisbury Plain, South Georgia*

We went ashore off the *Explorer* onto the beaches of Salisbury Plain, which lies on the north coast of South Georgia. We landed in Zodiacs, rubber boats with an outboard engine that seat about twelve passengers. The sea was relatively calm, patches of blue sky overhead, apparently quite rare in those climes. In 1777 Sir James Cook wrote of the island: "Lands doomed by Nature to perpetual frigidness: never to feel the warmth of the sun's rays; whose horrible and savage aspects I have no words to describe . . . the wild rocks raised their lofty summit til they were lost in the clouds and the vallies laid buried in everlasting snow. Not a tree or a shrub was to be seen, no not even one big enough to make a toothpick."

We wear inflatable life preservers, flat against our chests but which balloon open on being submerged in the water, and on top of them bright red parkas that against the snow stand out like red poppies. The Zodiacs are positioned to coast in on a wave, and we move to the rounded bow to swing our legs over and step into the swirl of receding water.

The island is about one hundred miles long, cucumber-shaped, twenty-five miles wide, indented with coves and bays. The mountains rise up abruptly from the shoreline; in the center of the island, permanently snow-capped, they rise as high as 9,000 feet. The northern coast has deep fjords and bays, protected from the winds, and thus perfect harbors for first the sealing and then the whaling industries. Captain Cook remarked on the fur seals (he referred to them also as "sea bears"), and ten years later the sealers arrived; a century later the species had been virtually exterminated. We are told only fourteen survived.

King Penguins

A colony of King Penguins on Salisbury Plain, South Georgia Island, numbers more than 70,000. The second largest penguin (next to the Emperor), in chorus they sounded (to me) like thousands of musicians playing kazoos.

What a testimonial to recovery! These days the fur seals crowd the beaches and the steep hills. One can spot their dark heads a hundred feet up against the green of the tussock. Quite aggressive too, as if they harbor a gene that tells them that these beings coming ashore off rubber boats in bright red parkas were up to no good in the time of their forebears and aren't now. Our leaders carried long sticks to ward them off. They run on the elbows of their flippers almost as fast as a man if they have a mind to, and we were warned to stay well clear. Just in case, we were asked to pick up two stones, and deposit them in our parka pockets, one to each side. If a seal makes a dash for us, the idea is to take the two stones out, not to throw them, one after the other, the most futile of gestures, but to clap them together, like a pair of miniature cymbals. The sharp sound, so we are told, hurts the seals' eardrums and stops them in their tracks. No one was quite sure of this; I suspect we would have preferred trading in the stones for the long sticks carried by our leaders. So we tended to give a wide berth to the fur seals lolling on the beach. They raised their dark otter-like heads and we increased the distance between us.

We were also told to keep clear of the giant petrels that pick among the detritus of the beach. They can vomit quite a distance, up to two meters, and they do this as an offensive weapon in that the vomit contains an oil made up of their last meal and a stomach fluid. It can mat an intruder's wing feathers—a skua, say—and indeed cause its death. It does not do this on the wing, thank goodness, although I don't see why it can't if it has a mind to.

Also on the beach are the elephant seals, inert, mammoth, four-ton sacks of blubber, sausage-shaped, lying in untidy heaps as if sleeping off a bad night. We saw no males with their proboscis noses that flop down over their lips and give them their name—just females, young adults. Apparently they do a considerable amount of belching and farting, but none of them in the heaps I walked by was moved to do so. They seem harmless. Back in the '90s a British sailor whose ship was in port at Grytviken made a bet that he could kiss an elephant seal on the lips. He crept up and tried it. He lost half a jaw, was put on a stretcher, and was invalided back home to England.

✧　✧　✧

The *Endurance* reached South Georgia Island on November 5, 1914, ten days after leaving Buenos Aires. On the third day out, a stowaway named Percy Blackborrow was discovered in a locker in the fo'c'sle. He was hauled before Shackleton, which led to a well-chronicled dialogue between the two. According to Frank Wild, Shackleton shouted at the boy, "Do you know that

Unlikely Pair
Here we have an elephant seal at rest and an inquisitive tussock bird, who doesn't worry about being consumed. Elephant seals feed predominately on squid, caught at astonishing depths (more than 1.5 miles) and, by slowing their heart rate to about a beat a minute, can stay down for about two hours.

Percy Blackborrow and Mrs. Chippy

Many of Mrs. Chippy's nine lives were used up when the cat jumped through a porthole into the sea on Sept 14, 1914, not long after *Endurance* left London's East India Docks. Hubert T. Hudson, the navigating officer, heard Mrs. Chippy's cries (it was a calm, still night) and turned the ship around to rescue the cat, who had spent about ten minutes in the water.

on these expeditions we often get very hungry, and if there is a stowaway available he is the first to be eaten?"

Not at all undone by this, the boy retorted, "They'd get a lot more meat off you, sir!" which won Shackleton's heart and just about everyone else's. He is listed in the ship's company rolls as "steward."

Before leaving for the Antarctic, the members of the Shackleton expedition were royally feted by the Norwegians on South Georgia—dinners at the station managers' so-called 'villas,' where the officials lived in grand style ... "replete with every comfort" as Shackleton wrote. The Grytviken Villa included "a billiard table, a piano, and a charming collection of geraniums blooming in the bow-windows." Frank Hurley, the ship's photographer, describes a "gramophone fling"—Scottish whalers from various stations treating the guests to a display of reels, jigs, and hornpipes ... the participants doubtless fortified by the moonshine of the whaling station, referred to as "plonk."

On their last night at South Georgia, the company was given what was rumored to be a costume party at the Grytviken Villa. One of the *Endurance* crew decided to come as a buddha and did so with what he had available—nothing but a sheet and a kettle-lid tied to his head. He was rowed ashore in a heavy snowstorm, half frozen when he arrived, only to discover that he was having his leg pulled; there was no costume party.

✧　✧　✧

JOURNAL ENTRY, 2002 • *En route to Albatross Island*

My hat blew off at Lat. 63, Long. 45 on the way to Albatross Island. I don't know if that is exact, but a classy notation nonetheless to set down in a notebook. I had just gone on deck to look for birds—petrels, skuas, albatross, and so on—and was watching a giant petrel keeping up with us abeam, barely moving his wings as he rode some unseen wind patterns, watching me, it seemed, as I was watching him, when the steady breeze sweeping along the ship's side somehow got under the brim of my hat and lifted it off before

I could get a hand up to fetch it back in. I went aft at the time and I could see it in the wake, a seabird white, and then it turned over in the tumbling waters and was gone. It was a golfing hat with "Redding Country Club" in red letters along the brim. I wasn't ever to wear it ashore—a deck-walking hat to keep my nose out of the sun. I remember feeling quite uncomfortable about losing it, the possibility of it floating about in the Antarctic ... ending up on a beach and lying there amongst the penguins, eventually to be discovered by some such as an ornithologist collecting data for the Cleveland Museum of Natural History.

This evening in my cabin I read the chapter in the latter pages of *Moby Dick* (under the title "The Hat") in which a "red-billed savage seahawk" swoops down and removes Ahab's hat and flies off with it ... "the wild hawk flew on and on with it; far in advance of the prow: and at the last disappeared; while from the point of that disappearance, a minute black spot was dimly discerned, falling from that vast height into the sea."

It's not quite identified, Melville's "seahawk," but the giant petrel fits, with its slightly reddish bill. I like to think that symbolically, at least, Ahab's hat is floating around down there, perhaps nudging my hat with the golf club's red stitching along the side.

✧ ✧ ✧

Whaling Home
The whaling station manager's house at Stromness Bay is now marked with a historical plaque. After leaving South Georgia, the next time Shackleton stood inside the manager's villa would be after emerging from the interior of the island following the wreck of the *Endurance*.

On the Ice
DECEMBER 1914—APRIL 1916

Shackleton's plan was to stay at Grytviken for only a few days before proceeding south. But the whalers informed him that the pack ice was further north than they could ever remember, a bad year, and they advised him to wait until the summer season was further along. So they waited a month; *Endurance* left Grytviken on December 5. The last sight those on board had of the whaling station through the morning mist was a drunken man reeling about on the quay. Only three days later, to Shackleton's surprise, *Endurance* reached the fringe of the pack ice as the whalers had warned—a disheartening sight since it meant finding a way through it for a thousand miles to reach their planned destination on the mainland at Vahsel Bay.

Sometimes *Endurance* had a good run through open water; at other times it was a slow push through the ice, looking for open leads. The ship was often accompanied by penguins, usually the Adélies. Their voices were recorded by Shackleton as sounding something like "Clark! Clark! Clark!" and since a member of the company, the biologist, bore that name, the standing joke when Clark took his turn at the wheel was that they all knew him, calling after him "Clark! Clark! Clark!" as the ship slipped through the ice. The Adélies also liked the singing of "It's a Long Long Way to Tipperary" (a popular song of 1912), but fled apparently when Leonard Hussey, a Londoner who had signed on as meteorologist, took out his banjo and played what Shackleton referred to as "music from Scotland."

An ominous sight on January 15 was a full-scale migration of crabeater seals in the many hundreds, porpoising as they passed the ship on their way north—indicating the extent of the pack ice. A possible landing on a large glacier was passed by. Shackleton kept pushing south. "Every mile we gain to the south means a mile less sledging when we come to start our great journey."

Finally, on January 19, the pack ice closed in around *Endurance*. Her forward motion ceased—only 67 miles from their intended landing point Vahsel Bay, and tantalizingly within sight of land. Shackleton wrote: "A survey of the position...showed that the *Endurance* was firmly beset. As far as the eye could reach from the masthead, the ice was packed heavily and firmly all around the ship in every direction."

So they were, as Frank Hurley put it, "trapped as a fly in a honey jar."

They began to drift north about a mile a day. Thomas Hans Orde-Lees, who had signed on from the Royal Marines, noted wryly that a year later they would be back where they started: "It certainly seems not improbable that we may remain...incarcerated [and] drift north, emerging about this time next year near South Georgia."

Shackleton set up a strict daily schedule to keep his men active in both spirit and body. Punctuality at all meals and at various events was insisted upon. A converted space in the hold for social gatherings, entertainments, and theatrics (it had a linoleum floor that Shackleton himself helped put down) was called the Ritz. The sailors aboard who bunked in the fo'c'sle were not invited to the theatrics because, as Orde-Lees wrote in his diary, "Our songs are mostly topical and some satirical. The sailors had to be satisfied with an ample tot of rum and gifts of sweets, fruits and tobacco which Sir Ernest provided them."

It would appear everyone had to perform, often to their dismay. The physicist on board, Reginald James, to general astonishment, provided great entertainment ("the gem of the evening," wrote skipper Frank Worsley) with a "Dissertation on the Calorie" as given by a short-sighted German professor named Herr Prof. von Schopenbaum. Dr. James McIlroy, the ship's second surgeon, did a daring impersonation of a semi-nude demi-mondaine Spanish danseuse, wearing an abbreviated dress made of velvet curtains, and wearing a blond wig.

Pack Ice

Shipmates aboard *Endurance* get their first view of pack ice as the ship proceeds south in December 1914. On his watch, Captain Frank Worsley delighted in ramming large floes at full speed and cutting them in two, enjoying the sensation as the ice gave way.

THE NAME GAME

O ne of the perquisites for being involved with Shackleton—financially, emotionally, or both—was getting memorialized on some piece of the Antarctic. Shackleton's most notable honorarium was undoubtedly the Beardmore Glacier, also known as "The Great Glacier." He named it for William Beardmore, the Clydesdale shipbuilder who helped finance the *Nimrod* expedition. Some authorities believe the glacier was named for Elspeth Beardmore, the industrialist's young wife, with whom Shackleton carried on a long-running affair that her husband was surely aware of. Beardmore eventually grew tired of the threat to his marriage, as well as Shackleton's increasingly desperate financial situation, and by the time of the *Endurance* expedition he had ended his patronage; Elspeth had cut him loose as well.

Overlooking the Beardmore Glacier is Mount Donaldson, named after Isobel Donaldson, with whom Shackleton had an affair in 1907. Elizabeth Dawson-Lambton, who helped with the *Nimrod*

An aerial view of the Beardmore Glacier, a frozen estuary more than 100 miles long that empties onto the Ross Ice Shelf.

financing, got a glacier named after her that is even larger than the Beardmore's. Janet Stancomb-Wills, the adopted daughter of a tobacco millionaire, had a large jutting promontory named after her—appropriately enough, as she was described as an amply endowed woman who enjoyed wearing necklaces and pendants. She got a dividend in having one of the three boats that made the trip to Elephant Island named after her.

Finally there was Rosalind Chetwynd, an American-born actress who went by the stage name Rosa Lind. She and Shackleton, who was ten years older, carried on a torrid affair for years. By an odd coincidence, Shackleton's landing on South Georgia Island after his open-boat voyage in 1916 was in the lee of a promontory that had already been named Mount Rosa. Perhaps wanting to make sure that his own Rosa got billing, he named the small beach Cape Rosa.

Show Time

On Midwinter's Day, 1915, which celebrated the return of the sun over the horizon, a variety show was held in the Ritz. Orde-Lees, as the Reverend Dr. Bubblinglove, opened the show with a rousing welcome to Shackleton. According to McNeish's diary, the "concert" went on from eight until midnight.

Shackleton himself didn't enjoy this kind of hilarity. His way of dealing with sexual deprivation was by pretending women didn't exist. He disapproved of theatrical skits in which his men put on dresses and got themselves dolled up with paint. He believed it suggested a lack of discipline. One of Shackleton's own skits seems somewhat self-revelatory—one in which he pretended to be a successful explorer being feted by the crowned heads of Europe.

There were parlor games, Shackleton himself the champion at "animal, vegetable, or mineral?" On one occasion, Hurley gave a lecture on his travels, illustrated with slides—those with vegetation and trees being especially appreciated. There were gramophone nights, which all hands attended. Musical competitions took place, Shackleton often the winner by unanimous vote. Hurley describes his voice as being "quaint, vacillating between sharps and flats in a most unique manner." He adds, "Wordie, our ex-champion, renders an old favorite, 'The Gambolier' in a voice resembling the shrill tone caused by drawing a rasp across of a sheet of galvanised iron. Clark renders, with much applause, 'My Nut Brown Maiden' in a nasal supertenor, and I render 'Waltzing Matilda', in a melting dulcet tone one often hears a swaggie crooning when punching his frugal damper. It is astounding the musical talent we do not possess!"

I had to ask around to find out what "punching his frugal damper" meant. An Australian friend obliged, and it was not what I thought. Apparently, "swaggie" is an itinerant laborer, and what he is doing is kneading a kind of unleavened bread.

Every Saturday night it was the custom to drink to sweethearts and wives—a ceremony, according to Hurley, enacted with "much fervour." During a musical evening in the wardroom, Harry McNeish, the ship's carpenter, rather "overdid the toast" as Hurley described it, and apparently became "very quarrelsome and, going to the fo'c'sle created a disturbance, which, fortunately, was quelled before any serious harm eventuated."

On the long sunsets before winter set in, soccer games were played out on the ice. Dog team races were organized, with chocolates and cigarettes serving as currency for those who wished to bet on the outcome. Shackleton promised that the best of the dog teams would be chosen for what he referred to as the Big Journey. Even as they drifted north, the concept of crossing the continent still remained in their minds.

There were any number of side diversions. Once, Worsley ran out naked on a floe and had himself a brief snow bath—very brief because the temperature was twenty-nine degrees Fahrenheit below freezing at the time. He wrote in his diary: "Poor Crean who was taking his pups for their morning constitutional on catching sight of me naked in the snow nearly fainted—thinking I'd 'gone wrong in the napper.' Now everyone except myself, is sorry for me & say its a pity to see one so young go wrong!"

✧ ✧ ✧

JOURNAL ENTRY, 2002 • *Aboard the* Explorer: *The Weddell Sea*
That night at dinner my table got talking about morale and how it would be kept up in situations like the *Endurance's*. Someone said that Admiral Byrd, the Antarctic explorer who led a mammoth expedition to the Antarctic in the '20s, believed that to keep morale high a leader should remain aloof—that the men should believe that their leader was somehow different, superior to them whether in fact he was or not. On one of his expeditions he brought along a morale officer who believed that spirits would

Dog Show
Tom Crean holds an armful of pups born on January 7, 1915, and photographed a month later. By August the pups weighed seventy pounds apiece, and Crean tried to train them to pull a sledge. Worsley wrote: "They pursue a devious and uncertain course…each pup possesses the voice of Jeremiah, his paunch is the paunch of Falstaff, and they flounder, puff and pant along through the snow…"

remain high if everyone learned to play the ukulele. So he brought along boxes of ukuleles... strumming the instruments, he believed, would keep everyone from becoming morose or homesick.

While everyone was laughing at the thought of a hundred or so ukuleles being strummed at the same time, someone asked if in the pursuit of participatory journalism I had ever been a ship's captain. I leaned back and after a pause to add a jot of suspense I said that I had—for one day I had been designated the captain of the *Vistaford*, a cruise ship of the Norwegian-American line. At the time the liner was in the Tasman Sea on the way around the world. I had joined her in Wellington, New Zealand, to give a lecture or two. The captain thought it might amuse the passengers, and provide a change in the ship's regimen if I took over on an informal basis. "You can have her for twelve hours," was how he put it.

I told the table that my first act as captain was to get on the loudspeaker system (connected to every stateroom, cabin, lounge, and dining room on the ship) and announce as follows: "Attention, please. This ship has been taken over." I mentioned my name and then I said, "As your captain, I feel I should tell you that I have some good news and some bad news. The good news is that the weather is going to be fine for the next few days, the wind out of the southwest at five knots. The bad news is that I have no idea where we are."

Someone at the table asked, "What time was it when you did this?"

"Seven A.M." I said. "I was on the bridge at the time, the captain quite nervous, as you can imagine, standing next to me, so I have no *personal*

Antarctica Revisited

In 1947, old-timer Richard Byrd returned to his Little America Hut on Antarctica. From there in 1929 Byrd made the first flight over the South Pole. He had arrived with ninety-five dogs (on the advice of Amundsen, then nearing his sixties), two ships and three aircraft. "The Pole," Byrd wrote, "lies in the centre of a limitless plain. And that is almost all there is to say about it. It is the effort of getting there that counts."

knowledge of what went on in the dining room. I've sort of imagined that among the passengers dipping into their bowls of Grape-Nuts flakes there was a certain amount of wide-eyed consternation.

I told my friends at the table that we had a woman on board whose husband had been shot in a botched robbery in a local A&P somewhere in New Jersey. She kept to her cabin, meals served to her there, in mourning, of course, and a cause of some concern.

"So one afternoon," I said, "she was persuaded to come up on deck to go fishing."

"Fishing!"

I explained that I'd persuaded the captain to stop the ship (after all I was the captain *pro tem*) right there in the middle of the Tasman Sea to go fishing. I'd bought a whole bunch of fishing lines in Wellington, hooks and so on. I think it was just the thought of people standing along the rail fishing off an ocean liner that inspired me to do such a thing.

"And she came up?"

"The woman from New Jersey. Yes, the steward was able to persuade her. Someone handed her a line. We baited the hooks with boiled shrimp, bright red, that would have been served that evening at the cocktail hour. Those who had lines stood along the rail and looked down to see how their shrimp were doing.

"And the New Jersey woman."

"She was standing looking sort of glazed, staring out at to sea, holding the line without much interest, rather perfunctorily. What she didn't know was that we had doctored her line."

"Loaded it up."

"Exactly. The ship's galley had provided us with a large fish, the kind that appears on a big platter at a buffet, gutted, but we stuck an empty wine bottle inside to flesh it out. One of the crew down below stuck a hook firmly into its jaw and then, leaning out a porthole, gave her line a couple of tugs."

Midnight Sun
Across the pack ice of the Weddell Sea, the midnight sun shines over Antarctica during the long austral summer.

I tried to described the look of utter disbelief that came over her face as she began bringing the fish up over the rail. The bottle fell out, and the fish was awfully dead, but that hadn't made any difference.

"We saw a lot more of her after that. We had a ceremony that evening, the last act of my short reign as captain. I got as many as I could to put messages in empty wine bottles. We gathered at the stern at a specific time, four o'clock whatever, and we threw the lot overboard. I've forgotten how many bottles, forty or so, and I remember the woman from New Jersey put a message in hers."

I didn't tell them this but I remember that afternoon the Tasman Sea was so calm, flat like a vast sheet of metal, that the thought crossed my mind that the clot of bottles would never disperse . . . that they would remain as we left them, on occasion clinking against one another in a slight swell . . . until finally a ship would come across them and out of curiosity the captain would stop and haul the lot aboard. Nothing much of interest, though. I had kept

Pool Hall

A multitude of diversions went on in the so-called Ritz—Sweethearts and Wives Night every Saturday (songs, toasts), gramophone concerts every Sunday, and even a billiards game on a miniature table.

duplicate strips of paper of what had gone into the bottles, a magnum of champagne to be awarded at the gala that night to the most original. Almost all the messages were affectionate notes to grandchildren, sorely missed, hoping that schoolwork was going well and so on. I don't recall the woman from New Jersey's message. I had put one in a bottle myself. It read: "Captain William Bligh is an old fart!" I signed it Fletcher Christian.

✧ ✧ ✧

One tends to get interested in the peripheral characters aboard *Endurance*. McNeish, the cantankerous carpenter, a problem with drink; Blackborrow, the young stowaway; Hurley, the photographer; Hussey and his banjo. One of these who certainly caught my fancy was Orde-Lees, surely the most eccentric of Shackleton's men, and rather a thorn in his side. Orde-Lees is mentioned only once, and that in someone else's words, in Shackleton's memoir, *South*. Orde-Lees came to *Endurance* from the Royal Marines. He had served briefly in China during the Boxer Rebellion and probably would have continued in the military service if he had not by chance heard a lecture given by Fridtjof Nansen, the legendary Norwegian explorer who in 1895 had established Furthest North (86' 16") after a mad dash following three years stuck fast in the pack ice aboard his ship *Fram*. (The word means "forward" in

Norwegian, which is ironic as the ship was in fact designed to be caught in the ice.) Orde-Lees decided on impulse that polar exploration was what he wanted to do. He rode up to London on a motorcycle, and he and Shackleton went in to see Churchill in the Admiralty, to ask if Orde-Lees could be transferred from the Royal Marines to Shackleton's command, which indeed was done.

But Orde-Lees, it would seem, was not the best of choices. He had invariably rubbed his shipmates the wrong way. In his early naval career, he annoyed them so much that they tied a rope around his waist and threw him overboard from a moving destroyer; he was so damaged by the experience that he had to spend the next six weeks in a hospital.

Nonetheless, some of his background seemed useful: he was an expert skier and mountain climber. He was a mechanic of sorts with motorcars—a device that was thought to have potential value in the snows.

But always his eccentricities got in the way. He brought a bicycle aboard *Endurance,* tried it on the ice without much success, although he could apparently do tricks with it, some species of wheelies, I would suppose. On one occasion he bicycled away from the ship and got lost; a search party had to go after him. Ordered not to leave the ship alone, he mourned in his diary: "No one knows what it means to me to have a bicycle and a place to ride it, however rough & heavy the going."

Splendid character. Some called him "Colonel," others "Old Lady," still others, "Peggy." A Peggy is the shipboard name for a person responsible for domestic labor, cleaning up and forth; in Lees's case, it was in reference to his old-womanish manner. Even Mrs. Chippy, the cat (according to his "diary" compiled by Caroline Alexander), had very little liking for Lees, referring to him on one occasion as "stupid." Mrs. Chippy remarks that Orde-Lees was the most disliked man on board ship, the butt of jokes, and couldn't seem to make friends. A Hurley photograph shows a long face, extended by a goatee, and with the earflaps raised up on his skiing hat; he looks quite like (as Mrs. Chippy points out) a large mouse.

Poor Orde-Lees. Even in sleep he was a target. One night when Hussey and Hurley were on the night watch, they were distracted from their chess match by Orde-Lees's snoring. In his diary, Hurley describes their attempt to cure what he refers to as "habitual." "Asleep on his back, with his mouth wide open, the gap seemed to invite a joke. Hussey, refreshing himself on sardines, suggested filling Lees's mouth with the tin, but I, more humanely,

ROSHOMON

1915
• Japanese writer Akutagawa Ryunosuke publishes *Rashomon,* a novel in which a murder is explained in several different ways. The book will have a huge influence on literature and films. Akira Kurosawa's 1950 film of the novel introduces Western audiences to Japanese cinema.

Yes Man

Orde-Lees was known for being too anxious to please Shackleton. One shipboard skit about him went: "Yes sir, oh yes certainly sir, sardines sir, yes sir here they are (dashes to pantry and back) and bread sir, oh yes sir, bread sir…".

dropped in several fish. The sardines disappeared, but the snoring increased and the mouth opened wider, perhaps in anticipation. Lentils, however, being nearby, I emptied a handful into the cavern with satisfactory results. We were able to proceed, without the diversion snores, with our game of chess."

Orde-Lees's diary is full of idiosyncratic observations, many of them self-revealing: "I am able to put aside pride of caste in most things but I must say that I think scrubbing floors is not fair work for people who have been bought up in refinement." At one point, though, because Green, the cook, had fallen ill, Orde-Lees found himself cooking for everyone on board, mainly because his mumbled statement to Shackleton that he couldn't and wouldn't cook was taken as an assent. He mourns: "Oh why oh why did I let my lying tongue run riot … If I ever did really boast that I could cook I merely meant … camp cookery for one or two people, but that I could cook a three course dinner for a whole ships company of 28 men—no, I never said I could do that & moreover I can't & won't do it. I'll either starve them or poison them."

Galley Duty

Charles Green, the ship's cook, at work carving up a seal for the evening's dinner. Despite its slightly gruesome nature, it was Green's favorite picture and the one he autographed and gave away as souvenirs following his lectures.

With the help of Blackborrow, the stowaway, he not only proved a competent cook, but more importantly was also able to get the ship's company to eat seal, even to prefer it to such delicacies as tinned rabbit. He did this through a ruse … by cooking seal mixed with masses of onions, its odors drifting enticingly throughout the ship. When one of the crew from the fo'c'sle asked what it was that they smelt cooking, Orde-Lees replied, "Oh, only some seal … for the wardroom"—where the officers dined.

"Well, if the wardroom can have it, we can, can't we?"

"Which would you rather have then, the seal or the rabbit?" Orde-Lees asked, and to his relief the crewman asked for the seal, and from that point on his mates preferred it to the tinned meat.

His diary is expressive, the liveliest of all, full of theories and ideas—one of them, I thought, astonishingly prescient. Imagining what explorers in the year 2015 would have as equipment, he wrote, "If there is anything less to explore, will not only carry their pocket wireless telephones … filled with

wireless telescopes but will also receive their nourishment and warmth by wireless." He prophesied that there would be daily excursion flights to both poles and that the goal of explorers would be the center of the earth.

On his return from the *Endurance* expedition, he campaigned to get pilots in the Royal Flying Corp (later the RAF) supplied with parachutes...to do away with the ridiculous idea fostered by the senior officers of the time that to do such a thing would rob the pilots of their fighting spirit and was, besides (like trekking with dogs), unmanly. Best to end up *splat!* To publicize his campaign, Orde-Lees took a successful parachute jump off Tower Bridge into the Thames. He became a Catholic, and went to see the Pope in Rome. He eventually married a Japanese woman, settled first in Japan, then in New Zealand. During the World War II, he became a spy. Caroline Alexander tells me that he was eminently suited to be a spy, but I'm not so sure—in a profession where one is supposed to blend in, he was hardly one to even attempt such a thing. He died at seventy-nine in a mental hospital. The cause of death was noted as "broncho-pneumonia—24 hours. Cardio-vascular degeneration. Senility?" They weren't sure. As Alexander writes: "Evidently, even the attending doctors could not quite get a handle on him."

The *Endurance* drifted north with the ice in the Weddell Sea for nearly 650 miles. There were intimations of what was going to happen. The ice was nothing like what we associate with a winter-time millpond. It seemed to have a life of its own, hummocks emerging, bergs shifting, tall tilts of ice rising up like vast tombstones. The pressure kept closing in on *Endurance* like a vise. The contours of her hull, straight rather than rounded like *Fram's*, did not allow her to ride above it.

A fateful moment occurred on July 14. McNeish recorded it as follows: "All hands is standing bye we had a slight shock last night...there was a noise under the bottom aft the same as if the ice had broken up...the Boss thinks it was a whale but I thinks different."

Frank Wild, the captain of *Endurance*, and Worsley happened to be in Shackleton's cabin when the ship quivered from the shock. Shackleton knew better, that it wasn't a whale. He said to his captain, "The ship can't live this, Skipper...You had better make up your mind that it is only a matter of time...what the ice gets, the ice keeps." He warned others that there was

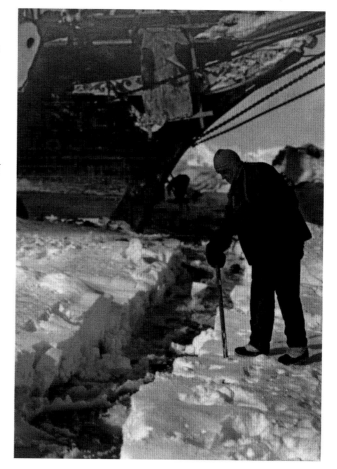

A Short Sail

On October 14, 1915, the ice split ahead of *Endurance* with a rumbling crash that brought everyone on deck. After a small sail called the spanker was set, the ship sailed for about 100 yards before coming to a halt in a lead blocked ahead by icebergs. Here Shackleton examines where the floe cracked ahead of the ship.

Worsley

Frank Worsley, the ship's captain, was a New Zealander who claimed to be part Maori. Although a skilled navigator, he was not, according to Shackleton, "the type to hold men well together."

Listing to Port

This photo by Frank Hurley shows how the pack ice had pinned *Endurance* and was slowly twisting her apart. At this point the men were preparing to abandon ship for the ice.

worse to come with the story of the mouse empowered with rum who imperiously inquires, "Now, where's that damned cat?"

The death of the ship was protracted. The diaries and memoirs describe the slow disintegration of her structure. The iron plates on the floor buckled up and overrode each other with loud clangs. The ship's beams cracked like pistol shots. Outside, the moving of the ice sounded like the roar of distant surf. Reginald James thought it sounded like the London traffic. The dogs were apparently sensitive to outside influences...a frenzy of barking in their pens when killer whales would surface in pools off the ship's side. They seemed aware that the *Endurance* was in trouble—releasing distressed choruses of woe and fear when the ice began to crush her sides. Worsley's diary mentions eight penguins that appeared on the ice floe. They seemed to be observing the ship, and began a curious keening. Worsley wrote: "I myself must confess that I have never, either before or since, heard them make any sound similar to the sinister wailings they moaned that day. I cannot explain the incident. I don't mind admitting that it was one of the queerest, and also one of the most disquieting, things that had hitherto happened to me."

The ice seemed to have a near-maniacal power, as Hurley's diary describes: "We began to rise from the ice, much after the manner of a gigantic pip squeezed between the fingers. In the short space of seven seconds, we were shot from the floes and thrown over to port, with a list of 30 degrees. All unsecured gear immediately rolled over to the lee side. On deck, great was the chaos: dogs, kennels, sledges and emergency gear were thrown in an inextricable tangle on the port side...I could not help laughing hilariously at our seating accommodation in the wardroom at dinner this evening. We all sat on the floor, with our feet jammed against lathes, to prevent sliding, and looking like the gallery of a music hall in Topsy Turveydom. One dare not rest anything on the table, or the 30 degree list immediately admonished you. What a ludicrous sight to observe the steward balancing and passing the plates of soup to the gallery, occasionally one would put down an empty plate or vessel on the floor—away it would careen to the port side."

When it was evident the ship was soon to founder, it became a matter of getting everything off her that would be of use on the ice...stores, sledging gear, clothing. Each man was allowed to keep only two pounds of personal possessions. In a graphic display of how only essentials were to be salvaged, Shackleton flung a handful of gold sovereigns, and his gold watch, out onto a pile on the floe to demonstrate what he thought was superfluous. To the pile

he added his silver brushes and his carrying cases. In a most dramatic gesture, he showed the assembled group the Bible which had been presented to the ship by Queen Alexandra, and lay it on the ice. He had ripped out the fly leaf, the Twenty-Third Psalm, and some verses from Job. Hussey wrote in his diary: "Thank God my old Banjo is safe." Hurley's last visit on board, hastened by the "portentous creaking around him," was to bring off in triumph a number of toothbrushes and toothpaste. Even the ship's pets were destroyed. On October 29 Shackleton wrote: "This afternoon Sallie's three youngest pups ... and Mrs. Chippy, the carpenter's cat, have to be shot. We could not undertake the maintenance of weaklings under the new conditions. Macklin, Crean, and the carpenter seemed to feel the loss of their friends rather badly."

About the same time Shackleton ordered the pets killed, he talked to Hurley about his photographic negatives, that perhaps they should go down with the ship since their weight and bulk would compromise any operations after the ship had gone. But Hurley was determined to save the record of his year's work. He kept a photograph album of developed snapshots called the Green Album. He went below into the mushy ice of the half-filled hold and, waist-deep, fished around in the semi-darkness to retrieve what he could. Luckily, the glass plates were stored in cases which were zinc-lined and soldered at the seams. He managed to bring over 550 to the surface. Out on the ice, he sorted through the lot and picked 150 of the best and smashed the rest, thus removing the temptation to add more to his selection. He kept only his pocket camera and three rolls of film.

A last meal was had in the wardroom. As they ate, the men could hear the sound of giving timbers rising from below. A clock was ticking in the wardroom when they left for the last time.

Shackleton wrote, "After times when hope beat high and times when the outlook was black indeed, the end of *Endurance* has come. But though we have been compelled to abandon the ship, which is crushed beyond all hope of ever being righted, we are alive and well, and we have stores and equipment for the task that lies before us. The task is to reach land with all the members of the Expedition. It is hard to write what I feel. To a sailor his ship is more than a

Dog Watch

This is one of Frank Hurley's best known and most reproduced photographs. In his book *South*, Shackleton captioned it "The End." A day or so later the mainmast was cut away so that salvage operations could begin in relative safety.

floating home, and in the *Endurance* I had centred ambitions, hopes, and desires. Now straining and groaning, her timbers creaking, and her wounds gaping, she is slowly giving up her sentient life at the very outset of her career."

At five o'clock in the afternoon of November 21, 1915, the wreck finally went down. Hurley notes, "The stern rose vertically, and a few minutes later, dived beneath the surface of the floe. We are not sorry to see the last of the wreck, for we have rifled it of everything likely to be of value to us, apart from being an object of depression to all who turned their eyes in that direction…"

Orde-Lees, in his inimical way, writes that Shackleton turned to him and said, "We've got it in the neck all right this time, haven't we?"

" 'Well, no. I don't think so,' I ventured. 'You wouldn't have anything to write a book about, if it hadn't been for this.'

" 'By Jove, I'm not so sure you aren't right,' he remarked [at] which we both had a good laugh."

One whaleboat and two cutters were taken off from *Endurance* in the early stages of the disembarkment to the ice. Shackleton named the largest, twenty-two feet in length, *James Caird*, the others *Dudley Docker* and *Stancomb Stancomb-wills*—all after the expedition's primary financial backers. The original idea was to march to a landfall to the northwest, hauling the boats along on sledges, but the drift of ice away from the shore and to the north made this impossible, and finally an encampment named Patience Camp was set up on an ice floe. Here they remained for three months, waiting for the the ice to break up in the southern summer.

McNeish had been very much opposed to the daily task of hauling the sledges across the ice, an opinion very likely strengthened by the fact that he suffered from a severe case of hemorrhoids. His idea was to build a serviceable sloop from the timbers of the three boats (he was a skillful carpenter, after all) that would be capable of carrying everyone to safety when the ice broke up.

Across the Ice

As soon as the *James Caird* was taken off *Endurance* onto the ice, McNeish, the ship's carpenter, began building up the topsides and fitting her with a pump that Hurley had made. Here the men in traces are hauling the whaler to an open lead 250 yards from camp to test her in the water. In his diary Worsley writes that McNeish has conditioned her so that, "She could now, at a pinch, carry 29 men."

Ocean Camp

A group portrait taken outside Shackleton's tent with Shackleton and Frank Wild, his second in command, in the foreground. One suspects from the men's informal attitudes that Hurley yelled from behind his camera to get their attention for an instant before they turned back to the camp's work.

Obdurate and sulky, he felt so strongly about his plan that he refused to obey orders. He felt he could do this legally—that with the sinking of the *Endurance* the laws laid down in the Ship's Articles had lapsed and he was no longer required to obey orders.

Shackleton, as it happened, carried the Ship's Articles off the *Endurance*, the last thing in the world I would have thought of doing, and read them dramatically to all hands gathered on the ice floe. He recited the paragraph that reads that the crew must agree to commands whether on board, in the boats, or on shore—and that disobedience to commands was legally punishable.

McNeish backed down, but relations between the two were uncomfortable, at best. Shackleton does not mention the incident specifically in his book *South* except to note, "I shall never forget him in this time of strain & stress." He subsequently left him off the list of those who eventually received the prestigious Polar Medal.

Despite the trouble with McNeish, Shackleton refused to reserve the privileges a leader might have held for himself. "If he had half a pipe of tobacco," wrote a seaman named Water How, "he'd share it." Though he was referred to as "the Boss," he promoted the idea of equality among his men to make sure they remained a close-knit group. Of this Reginald James remembered, "I do not think there is any doubt that we owe our lives to his leadership and to his power of making a loyal and coherent party out of our diverse elements."

So the floe drifted north. Hurley wrote in his diary: "It is beyond conception, even to us, that we are dwelling on a colossal life raft, with but five feet of ice separating us from 2,000 fathoms [12,000 feet] of ocean and

drifting along under the caprices of wind and tide, to heaven knows where."

Worsley, who had climbed the spur of an iceberg, on viewing the tents on the ice floe below remarked on how much the encampment looked like a "collection of Indian wigwams."

Orde-Lees got into his usual troubles with Shackleton, in this case because he felt that every seal and penguin they spotted should be killed and added to the ice floe's stores. Shackleton opposed this on the grounds it would suggest a protracted stay on the floes, compromising morale. It turned out Orde-Lees was right. The food stores began to run out. A keen sense of the situation turns up in Shackleton's own memoir: "Another man searched for over an hour in the snow where he had dropped a piece of cheese the day before, in the hope of finding a few crumbs. He was rewarded by coming across a piece as big as his thumb-nail, and considering it worth the trouble."

Since the dogs consumed a seal's worth of food every day, Shackleton ordered them shot, team by team, as the days went by, greatly distressing the men. On January 14, four teams were shot, twenty-seven dogs in all. Wild, who was one of the executioners, wrote, "I have known many men I would rather shoot than the worst of the dogs." Hurley, who took loving portraits of all the dogs, in a wonderful section of the Green Album saluted his favorite dog, "Hail to thee old leader Shakespeare, I shall ever remember thee— fearless, faithful, & diligent."

Their aversion to eating dog was abandoned at this point. When the younger dogs joined the food supply, Hurley accepted this sad business and had wry fun with it in his journal: "Ate one of young dogs, tender, flavorous, especially Nelson, which equalled veal. Macabre scene in which the dog owners complain that their dogs, frizzing invitingly away on the grill, are getting mixed up with others. Gruss's owner, Macklin, complains that the cook is scorching Gruss... a casual observer might think the explorer a frozen-hearted individual, especially if he noticed the mouth watering when tears ought to be expected. Hunger brings us to the level of all other species, and our saying, 'that sledge dogs are born for work and bred for food' is but the rationale of experience."

A MOVEABLE FEAST

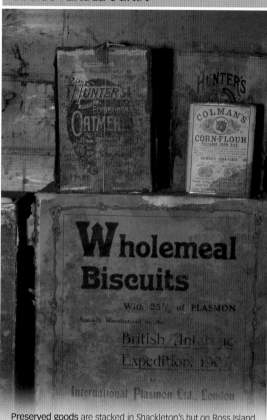

Preserved goods are stacked in Shackleton's hut on Ross Island. Biscuits were fortified with Plasmon, a form of milk protein.

Pemmican, ground dried meat mixed with fat, was the main course of a sledging party. It was the only proven concentrated foodstuff of the time and thus used on all the polar expeditions. Other items went along—chocolate, cocoa, sugar, cheeses—but the staple dish was pemmican and a hard biscuit. The pemmican tins were opened and the contents dropped into a pot set on the Primus stove, a little water (from melted ice or snow) added, and the resulting stew concoction was called, at least by English explorers, "hoosh." Sometimes other items, like oatmeal, were added to the hoosh. One hoosh described by the *Endurance's* photographer, Frank Hurley, consisted of penguin legs, livers, and hearts.

I remember reading about a distinguished explorer who had mentioned pemmican to a lady and being startled by her inquiry, which was: "Well, what I don't understand is how you shoot them."

✧ ✧ ✧

JOURNAL ENTRY, 2002 • *Deception Island*

One of the vague possibilities that Shackleton had in mind as the floes drifted north was somehow sledging to open water and reaching Deception Island, over a hundred miles to the west.

The island is, in fact, a flooded volcano, shaped like a doughnut with a small bite taken out of it. The narrow entrance where a piece of the rim collapsed and the sea rushed in is the wonderfully named Neptune's Bellows; the mountains rise abruptly on either side of the entrance through which the winds, usually in the Antarctic winter, on occasion funnel through at hurricane-like speeds. Once through, though, any ship moves into sheltered waters. In the 1900s the caldera became a center of whaling activity. Port Fisher has a runway, a rust-encrusted hangar, tanks, pipes, lying about in a disordered clutter, rust-red against the lava black.

But the excitement of the place is the swimming. Here and there along the shoreline are so-called "fumaroles" created by geothermal activity. The passengers were urged to bring bathing suits, such an odd thought that when I received the notice in the mail back home I either dismissed it or thought it had to do with sunbathing on the foredeck of the *Explorer* in the feeble rays of the astral sun. So I crept into the water in my black long johns. Ten or fifteen of the passengers also went in, including Charles Osgood, who is eighty-something, among the bird-watcher group, indefatigable, very spindly, sparrow-boned, creeping toward the water.

The temperature of the water along the shoreline is about 80 degrees but drops precipitously. Lying parallel to the shore, it's quite like being in a bath, but as soon as I swung my body out toward the open water, my legs entered an ice-bucket zone. I have swum in Maine where the temperature drops into the high fifties and knocks the breath out of you as you go in. Here the water knocks the life out of you, and very quickly. Sometimes a small wave would wash over those of wallowing at the waters edge; loud gasps from the men, high-pitched yells from the females along the line. Scalded and hypothermic at the same time. As I lay wallowing I recall thinking what a shame it was that Shackleton's people in the *James Caird* and the two cutters hadn't sailed

Watering Hole

At Deception Island, the sea has filled a dormant caldera surrounded by pumice slopes. Heat escapes from subterranean volcanic vents. Numerous eruptions have occurred, most recently in 1991 and 1992. In 1923 an eruption heated the water in the harbor to the boiling point and scalded the paint off ships' hulls.

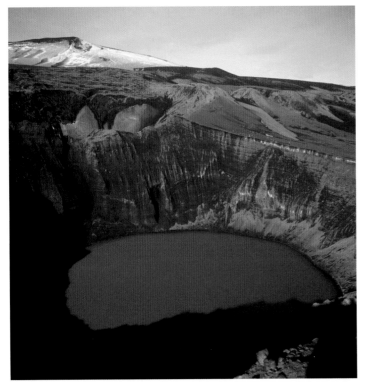

through Neptune's Bellows to luxuriate in the warm thermal springs while awaiting rescue, and how anticlimactic to the whole saga it would have been if they had.

A quarter of a mile down the beach is a low, corrugated steel aircraft hangar standing amidst the detritus (pipes, tanks, and the fuselage of a plane with its wings removed) of what was once a working airstrip. It was from here that the Australian Hubert Wilkins made the first powered flight in the Antarctic, taking off and flying for twenty minutes in a Lockheed Vega monoplane named *Los Angeles*.

In Lowell Thomas's biography of Wilkins he tells of a New Year's Eve celebration the aviator spent at Whalers Bay during which two drunken sailors climbed atop a pair of sperm whales swollen from the fermentation taking place in their bodies. When one of them thrust a knife into the whale the two were standing on, the whale exploded, hurling both into the harbor. Both men were pulled out before the hypothermia got to them. I would have guessed alcohol, the local bathtub booze known as plonk, may have been a factor in their survival.

Back on board the *Explorer* that evening, a message arrived via e-mail that my daughter had given birth to a girl, my first grandchild...who must have emerged into the world just about the same instant I emerged from the waters of Discovery Bay...not a coincidence of particular moment but interesting enough to tell her when she comes of that age when she can abide her grandfather's stories without falling asleep.

✧　　✧　　✧

So what did they talk about on the ice floes drifting north? Hurley gave us a partial list of favorite themes in his diary: comparison of the social life of London, New York, and Paris; population control; the birth rate; the liquor question; politics; and (by far the most popular) what Hurley refers to as "other lands and unknown places." Sometimes the topics seem quite specialized: The development of commerce on the Yangtse, or the arts and crafts of ancient Egypt. Then there were recitations of poetry, often Sir Ernest with his favorite passages of Browning, which he knew by heart. And Hussey's banjo was still with them.

Hurley records what he was reading—strange indeed what reading matter was taken off *Endurance* and thought to be "indispensable": "texts on Borneo cotton, Kinglake's *Eothen*? (I would rather carry this excellent book than six times its weight in rations)." He writes of how transfixed he is by the accounts of interminable desert sands, the Sphinx, the Great Pyramids, the olive groves of Damascus, and to turn from this to his icebound captivity under a leaden sky—and yet even here that optimism of his: "We know that beyond that horizon lies the great rolling road to freedom and so we look forward."

Arguments were solved by an inspection of the *Encyclopaedia Britannica*, one of the books they chose to lug along. Shackleton came upon two sailors in a very heated discussion on the subject of "Money and Exchange." They finally came to the conclusion that the *Encyclopaedia* must be wrong.

Frank Hurley was especially useful at Patience Camp. In addition to keeping up with his photography he built a stove that the entire company relied on for meals. He made a portable blubber stove for the boats. "Great success," he wrote. "Boiled 2 1/2 [gallons] from ice 1/2 hour." From the *Endurance*'s binnacle, the stand that had housed the compass, he made a pump eventually put aboard the *James Caird*.

Hurley's diary of the experience on the ice after *Endurance's* foundering is like none of the others. His descriptions of the icebergs, the pack ice, read like the most exalted passages from a travel brochure. Every day is "beautiful." He writes on the 23rd of February: "Providence is both considerate and kind. It would appear as if the evolution of the Penguin and Seal species had developed especially along lines calculated to fill the wants of Polar castaways. The blubbery layer of subdermal tissue of the seal is sufficient to convert his entire carcass into Roasts, Boils, and Hooshes . . . A seal is consumed by the entire party in 5 days—just as long as his blubber lasts. 20 Penguins cooked by the fuel of their skins is a fair daily average . . . Even our encampment is being born northwards on an immense much maligned ice raft, which we expect —(very remotely at present) to open up and be so condescending as to make a smooth water canal to our Haven. Albeit we have much to be thankful for (man is essentially a discontented animal). I have heard murmurs of tea being too strong and puddings too sweet. What hardships we (don't) have to endure. Secured two Weddells and massacred 130 Penguins. Beautiful day! Exquisite ski surface! Splendid wind! Three good meals and warm sleeping bags. Favorable report from the meteorologist."

As the days go by, other accounts speak of grim hardships, the lack of food in particular as their supplies began to dwindle. Hot drinks were rationed to one cup of tea a day. McNeish writes, "So there is nothing for it but get in our

Frank of All Trades

When Frank Hurley was not taking photos or filming, he tinkered around making all sorts of useful things—a weighing scales, a bilge pump, tools for salvaging operations, stoves. Here he sits beside a stove of his design, skinning a penguin for use as fuel. Reginald Green took the picture while the "Boss" sat alongside.

DRESS REHEARSAL

In Antarctica, even putting on articles of clothing could be a trial, especially a frozen boot. The method was to edge a foot into the top of the boot, de-icing it with body heat, then withdrawing the foot and rewarming by rubbing it briskly between the hands, then reinserting it into the chill of the boot, a process repeated over and over, often for hours, until finally the boot was supple enough to accept the entire foot. One can imagine the torture for anyone doing this who was already suffering from frostbite.

Even a sleeping bag that one could assume was a haven from the cold could be stiff as a misshapened suit of armor; to get into it required an agony of twisting and turning. Because the bag retained breath vapor and perspiration, it increased in weight. Cherry-Garrard in his journal records that at the start of a six-week journey, his sleeping bag weighed eighteen pounds; on their return, it weighed forty-five pounds.

A constant problem was humidity. The vapor condensed on the walls, froze at night, melted during the day... and mildew, which got into blankets and clothes, was the result. The explorer Otto Nordenskjöld writes of a pea that "found its way into my blankets and began to grow there. It had thrown out roots and a long stalk with embryo leaves—the latter a pale aenemic yellow since they had never seen the sun."

Robert Scott, prepared for any weather. The chest harness kept mittens from blowing away, which would mean horrible frostbite.

sleeping bags. And smoke away the hunger." Fortunately, at the end of February a flock of Adélie penguins popped up on the ice and three hundred were taken, providing not only food but fuel for heating. The Weddell seals turned up as well. Hurley remarked on them, "Unfortunate for you that your flesh is so excellent and your blubber burns so well!"

As they drifted north about two miles a day they suddenly caught a glimpse of land, Joinville Island, its jagged, snow-covered ridges the first sighting for sixteen months. As Hurley wrote about it, "If the ice opens up, we could land in a day." But the ice held them fast—the distant peaks a tantalizing sight on the western horizon as the three boats slid past. What was now on everyone's mind was that if the ice didn't break soon, the northbound current would sweep them past the tip of the peninsula out into the South Atlantic with no hope of survival. If the area between the fortieth and the fiftieth parallels of latitude is known familiarly as the Roaring Forties,

THE IRISH TROUBLES

April 1916
• Members of Ireland's Sinn Fein Society seize control of the Dublin Post Office, during an uprising against British rule. The bloody attack coincided with the arrest of Irish nationalist Roger Casement, who was caught trying to smuggle arms from Germany into Ireland. The rebel leaders eventually surrender.

Weddell Sea
On Patience Camp, the *Endurance* crew had to contend with a shifting landscape of ice. The iceberg in the distance across the pack ice of the Weddell Sea is tabular in shape and has broken away (calved is the proper terminology) from either the Ronne or the Filchner Ice Shelves, which form the Weddell's southern coast.

between the fiftieth and seventieth parallels is referred to as the Filthy Fifties—where the winds circling the globe in a continuous belt and unimpeded by any land mass create not only a zone of unremitting gales, but massive roller waves that can measure three quarters of a mile between their crests, with troughs of fifty feet. It was essential that Shackleton get his men off the ice and into the boats before the ice was pushed into such seas.

Undulating under their feet in the long rollers coming in from the north, the ice began to split and leads of water opened up. Their world, which had been a relatively smooth surface of pack ice, was now a massive field of acre-sized floes, jostling and butting each other in the swells. Shackleton envied the seals on the rocking floes. "They were at home and had no reason for worry or cause for fear. If they thought at all, I suppose they counted it as an ideal day for a joyous journey on the tumbling ice. To us it was a day that seemed likely to lead to no more days."

The ice split off and cracked, until finally Patience Camp rested on a triangular-shaped ice shelf only 100 yards at its widest. The situation had become so dire that Shackleton ordered the three boats launched into what Hurley described as "…a transcending view of an infinity of ice covered ocean-berg fragments, shattered floes and brash ice, heaving under the mighty influence of Cape Horn rollers and grinding, crunching, groaning into an an indescribable chaos. We viewed with anxiety this profound menace and when it seemed our floe must split under the rolling motion, the ice opened magically, the boats were launched and loaded, and we were free once more, vowing to remain all night drifting and rowing along pack margin, the swell having abated for snowing."

In the distance they could see the conical peaks of Clarence Island, about sixty miles away through the ice-strewn seas, but the three crowded boats, headed by Shackleton in *James Caird*, made little headway. The freezing spray coated both men and gear with ice, and finally they hauled up for the night on a piece of flat ice hoping that it would hold together until they left the next morning. On occasion, their worst fears were realized, as Shackleton remembered: "Some intangible feeling of uneasiness made me leave my tent about ll p.m. and glance around the quiet camp, and I started to walk across the floe to warn the watchman to look carefully for cracks, when as I was passing the men's tent the floe lifted on the crest of a swell and cracked right under my feet…The crack had widened to about 4 feet and…I saw a whitish object floating in the water. It was a sleeping bag with a man inside. I was able to grasp it, and, with heave, lifted man and bag on the floe. A few seconds later the ice-edges came together again with tremendous force."

The man in the bag was Holness, one of the fo'c'sle hands. He was extracted from the sleeping bag and walked up and down the ice floe by his mates to get his circulation going, his clothes coated with ice, crackling as he went. What seemed to bother him more than being dunked in the water was the fact that he'd lost his tobacco.

It would seem that the men would have welcomed the chance to be at sea again despite the cockleshell fragility of their craft, but at times they must have prayed for the icebound sanctuary of Patience Camp. Greenstreet described what it was like in the open seas: "One moment we were up on the tremendous crest of a swell—you could see right away to the horizon, nothing but sea and ice and sky—then you'd drop into the hollow and see a great roller coming toward you filled with blocks of ice."

A possible landfall on Clarence or Elephant Island seemed just a step around the corner compared to the distances they'd traveled, but they were beset by just about every terrifying condition possible—squalls, gale-force winds, fog, tumultuous seas, sub-zero temperatures, pack ice on the move—but what many of them remembered more than the rest was the fact they were accompanied by a number of killer whales. They had seen the whales rise up suddenly and with their heads break an ice floe apart to get at the seals; the thought of a sudden shivering blow lifting the boat in shards of splintered wood must have crossed their minds a multitude of times. Those aboard *Dudley Docker* were especially concerned: a single, big killer whale lounged alongside as if it had adopted them, just an oar's length away…its fin, its tip flopping over slightly, rose out of the sea taller than the heads of the men in the boat.

Orde-Lees was in the *Dudley Docker*. At first, he behaved, well, badly. He refused to row, as he said, because the seas were too rough or he was too cold, and besides he was a "rotten oarsman." He lay down in the bottom of the boat and was carried along like a passenger.

Safely Ashore

With his "Vest Pocket" Kodak, Hurley stepped into the shallows to record the men hauling the *James Caird* clear of the water, with the *Stancomb-Wills* and the *Dudley Docker* in the foreground. The night before, the *Dudley Docker* had been separated from the others in a snow squall, and only reappeared just as Shackleton was about to land. The men in the smaller cutters suffered terribly. One of them from the *Stancomb-Wills* went half-crazy and killed ten seals before he stopped. Clearly visible to the left of the boats is Percy Blackborrow, crippled by frost bite.

But then suddenly he redeemed himself (could it have been the killer whale's fin looming over him?) and indeed can be credited with keeping *Dudley Docker* from going under. Seas kept collapsing over her gunwales. He grabbed a bucket and went to work. He was fresher than anyone else on board, very likely because he had sworn off rowing, and his tireless windmilling use of a bucket, filling it and emptying it overboard, kept the situation under control. And that wasn't all. When Greenstreet's feet became frostbitten, Orde-Lees put them between his tunic and his bare stomach, bared to the cold, to warm them up, hardly an act one would think of from such a patrician. Even so, presumably because the ice-cold affected his stomach, he writes in his diary "...I cursed myself for a Samaritan."

Finally a suggestion of doom creeps into Hurley's diary: He writes, "Last night, a night of tension & anxiety—on a par with the night of the ship's destruction...Sea & wind increase & have to draw up onto an old isolated floe and pray to God it will remain entire throughout the night. No sleep for 48 Hours, all wet Cold & miserable with a N.E. Blizzard raging...no sight of land & Pray for a cessation of these wild conditions."

Diarrhea was endemic from eating uncooked pemmican. Sufferers settled their buttocks over the gunwales, holding onto ropes, or being held on to by shipmates to keep from going overboard in heavy seas; they used slivers of ice to clean themselves.

And always the cold. Worsley wrote, "It was so cold that our Burberry overalls cracked, and ice and frost fell off us as we rowed. When the moon

LUSITANIA TORPEDOED

May 8, 1915
• United States neutrality in World War I is strained when two torpedoes from a German submarine sink the British ocean liner *Lusitania*, killing 124 Americans on board. The Cunard Line ship, bound from New York for Liverpool, sank just ten miles off the coast of Ireland.

came out, we saw that our beards were white with frost, moustaches were knobbed with ice, and each man's breath formed clouds of vapor, showing white against the darkness of his face."

At the very last, ten miles from the coast of Elephant Island, slightly closer at hand than Clarence Island, the three boats ran into a strong current that held them in place as if they were once again entombed in ice. After an hour of rowing as if their lives depended on it, which indeed was so, they had not moved closer. A storm broke and they spent another night in lumpy seas, their sixth on the water. Shackleton's leadership held them together, calling across to the other boats words of encouragement or praise, always in command. At nine the following morning, after skirting cliffs in a heavy mist, they spotted a narrow beach. Shackleton had not slept since Patience Camp a week before. His tongue and lips were so swollen that he could only whisper his orders. He transferred to the *Stancomb-Wills* to take her in first. The cutter rode in on the crest of a wave, her keel grating against the stones.

Then a strange moment. Shackleton decided on impulse that the first one to step ashore on Elephant Island should be the youngest. "…I told Blackborrow to jump over. He seemed to be in a state almost of coma and in order to avoid delay I helped him, perhaps a bit roughly, over the side of the boat. He promptly sat down in the surf and did not move. Then I suddenly realized what I had forgotten that both of his feet were frost-bitten badly. Some of us jumped over and pulled him to a dry place. It was a rather rough experience, but, anyhow, he is now able to say he was the first man to sit on Elephant Island."

As for the rest, Reginald James reported that, "most of us hardly knew whether to laugh or cry…we took childish joy in looking at the black rocks & picking up the stones, for we had not stepped on land since Dec. 5, 1914."

Hurley wrote about his fellows that they reeled about as "if they had found an unlimited supply of alcoholic liquor on the desolate island. … Many suffered from

Adélie Penguins

The Adélie penguin (here on Elephant Island) was named after the French explorer Dumont d'Urville's wife. Adélies and emperor penguins (the largest of the species) are the only ones found solely on the Antarctic continent.

temporary aberration, walking aimlessly about, others shivering as if with palsy—for the results of five days and nights without sleep or rest in frozen garments, combating the fierce anger of the Southern Ocean in winter, must needs pay it[s] tribute. Tents were hastily erected and after partaking of a meal of delicious seal steaks all turned in, and almost instantly were deep in slumber. How delicious to wake in one's sleep, and listening to the chanting croaks of the penguins mingling with the music of the sea. To fall asleep and awaken again, and feel this is real. We have reached the land; and that our latitude and longitude will remain the same on the morrow."

In his book *The Worst Journey in the World*, Apsley Cherry-Garrard writes a memorable portrait of Shackleton at this particular moment of crisis off Elephant Island: "A picture haunts my mind—of three boats crammed with frost-bitten, wet, and dreadfully thirsty men who have had no proper sleep for many days and nights. Some of them are comatose, some are on the threshold of delirium or worse. Darkness is coming on, the sea is heavy, it is decided to tie off the cliffs and glaciers of Elephant Island and try and find a landing with the light . . . man would have tried to get a little rest in preparation for the coming struggle. But Shackleton is afraid the boat made fast to his may break adrift . . . All night he sits with his hand on the painter [the rope that connects the three boats], which grows heavier and heavier with ice as the unseen seas surge by, and as the rope tightens and droops under his hand his thoughts are busy with future plans."

A Hot Meal

Heated up on Hurley's stove, this meal was the first sustenance for the men in three-and-a-half days. It was the first time they had set foot on land in 497 days. From left to right: Orde-Lees, Wordie, Clark, Rickenson (who would later suffer a heart attack), Greenstreet, How, Shackleton, Bakewell, Kerr, and Wild.

The Voyage of the *James Caird*

APRIL—MAY 1916

Elephant Island is about 23 miles long, 13 miles at its widest, almost entirely made up of crags and glacier-laced mountains rising steeply out of the sea, offering very little in the way of beaches or shelter. The first beach the castaways had landed on was so exposed that after one day the group moved to a safer haven about seven miles down the coastline. It came to be known as Cape Wild, after Frank Wild, whom Shackleton put in charge, often referred to as Camp Bloody Wild. A bleak and forbidding place, just an acre or two of rock and shingle, with the sea foaming around except where the snow-slope ran up to a glacier and formed the landward boundary. It had its advantages—drinking water from the glacier, a penguin colony nearby. The camp was, in fact, situated on top of a past colony, which meant that once the snow underneath their various tents had melted they found themselves atop a reeking surface of penguin guano.

On April 19, two days after their arrival at the new camp, Shackleton gathered his men around him to announce his plans. What he didn't tell them was that probably the most logical thing to do would be to wait it out on Elephant Island throughout the winter and escape in the spring to the south toward Deception Island and the whaling stations in the area. He had discussed this with Wild and Worsley; all three felt that the mood of the men, especially the crewmen from the foc's'le, was so low and dispirited, a kind of "What's the use?" attitude, that it was

A LINE IN THE SNOW

The Royal Navy officers from the second Scott expedition prepare to meet the King at Buckingham Palace in 1913. Napoleonic-style uniforms were part of British naval tradition.

Very likely because of his service in the merchant marine rather than the rigidly hierarchical Royal Navy, Shackleton was noted for his egalitarian stance with his men. Although he expected discipline and the following of orders (and was capable of reacting strongly when orders were disregarded), he had no interest in acting superior. But he was the exception. The separation between officers and crew members in those times could hardly be more graphically illustrated than by the standards set by Lt. Victor L. Campbell, whose six-man recconaissance group from Robert Scott's *Terra Nova* expedition was trapped for the winter in a nine-by-twelve-foot ice cave. Campbell drew a line with the sole of his boot in the snow to signify separate quarters. He pointed to one side and said, "That becomes the mess deck," and then to the other: "This will be the quarterdeck." Neither side was to eavesdrop on the other.

The arrangement was described by a member of the party, the geologist Raymond Priestley, who wrote: "Commander Campbell knew that our enlisted men had come up from the ranks in the Royal Navy. They had been in it since they were young boys, and he knew they would be uncomfortable with too much familiarity with the officers and the loss of the sense of belonging to the messdeck. From that day onward, each of us knew exactly where he stood and this contributed enormously to our tranquility."

preferable, since there was no hope of rescue from the outside world, to take action and go for help themselves.

There were three possibilities—Tierra del Fuego, 600 miles away to the northwest at the tip of South America; Port Stanley in the Falklands, the closest, about 550 miles due north; and then South Georgia, a little under 800 miles to the northeast. Because of the difficulty of heading up into the prevailing westerly currents and winds, the only feasible choice was to set out for South Georgia.

Shackleton told them this, that he would be taking the *James Caird,* and asked for volunteers. There were not many. Some, still recovering from their travails on the open ocean, never wished to get into a small boat again. Others thought the plan had no hope of succeeding. Orde-Lees was one of the latter. "I decided to excuse myself."

Shackleton himself warned them: "Better a living dog than a dead lion."

To get the *James Caird,* the largest of the craft, ready for the voyage, McNeish, the carpenter, cannibalized the other two. He built up the gunwales from wooden supply cases, planks from the *Dudley Docker,* and the mast from the *Stancomb-Wills* to fortify the keel so the boat wouldn't break up in the pounding of the seas. He covered the deck with canvas, leaving an opening hatch framed with pieces of wood with just enough room, four feet by two feet, for a couple of heads to look out at the same time. The work was completed in four days. To go with him, Shackleton picked Frank Worsley as the navigator; two seamen, Thomas Crean and Tim McCarthy; the bo'sun Vincent; and McNeish, the latter choice somewhat of a surprise because of the unpleasantness at Patience Camp on the ice floe. McNeish was delighted. He had volunteered to go. Considering a winter on Elephant Island, he had said, "I don't think there will be many survivors."

Every morning at daybreak he worked on the *Caird;* he finished her to his satisfaction on April 24. She was launched and promptly began to fill with water. It was then discovered that the bottom plug had been forgotten—but the fact that she had to be bailed out before she'd even started was not the best of omens.

Riding light, she was rowed out and anchored a hundred yards offshore while ballast and supplies were ferried out to her on the *Stancomb-Wills.* Shackleton smoked a last cigarette with Wild, shook hands with everyone staying behind, and then pushed off in the *Stancomb-Wills* to board the waiting *Caird.*

Patch Job

On April 20, 1916, carpenter McNeish began dismantling the *Dudley Docker,* using its wood to deck in the *James Caird* for the open boat journey. On the barren beach the nearest tree was a thousand miles away. Improvisation was the order of the day. The seams of the *James Caird* were caulked with lamp wick and the artist George Marston's oil paints.

Strong Man
Shackleton thought John Vincent (here mending a net), would prove physically to be the strongest aboard the *James Caird*. Moreover, he had a rather bullying manner which Shackleton felt might be unsettling if he were to be left behind in the close quarters of the Elephant Island contingent. So he took him along. But the ordeal of the voyage proved to be too much for him. It was not long before Vincent, in Shackleton's words, "ceased to be an active member of the crew."

They set sail that afternoon. Orde-Lees commented that the penguins in the nearby colony seemed to join in with their calls as the men stood on the shore waving their farewells. "We watched them until they were out of sight; which was not long, for such a tiny boat was soon lost to sight on that great heaving ocean; as she dipped into the trough of each wave she disappeared completely sail & all."

Once at sea, Shackleton divided those aboard into two three-man watches, four hours on, four hours off. One was put to duty at the steering, another to tend the sails, and the third at the hand pump. At the end of each watch the men who had been relieved would creep forward into an arrow-shaped area five feet in width and tapering for seven feet to where the planking joined at the bow. Packed together in their reindeer-skin sleeping bags, they slept fitfully in this cranny as the *Caird* lurched about in the seaway. In Worsley's words, "We were lifted up & hurled down & our bodies were whipped...flailed & stamped."

Meals were every four hours. "The worst feature of meals," Worsley said, "was that there was not enough headroom to sit upright. One has no idea before making the experiment how...distressing this is. The chest is pressed down on the stomach, one swallows with difficulty & the food appears to have no room to go down."

First, they sailed directly north so that they could head downwind with the prevailing westerlies for South Georgia.

The *Caird's* crew later described a never-ending series of critical situations—gales following upon gales, days spent hove-to, then endless bailing and pumping, and always facing the possibility of missing South Georgia entirely and being swept out once again into the wastes of the South Atlantic.

There are two remarkable passages that give a sense of what it must have been like. The first is Worsley's from his account *Shackleton's Great Boat Journey* and will have special meaning to anyone who has sailed a small craft with a big following sea rearing up over the stern. "In steering a small boat before a heavy gale, don't look back, it may disconcert you. Fix your eye with a glassy glare on a cloud or breaking sea right ahead & keep her straight, if you can.

When you hear a roaring Bull of Bashan with a wet nose galloping up behind you keep your head well forward & your shoulders hunched up to your ears—till you get it."

The other is Shackleton's from *South*—a glimpse into the optimistic side of his nature, that whatever the odds the chances were they would pull through: "[I] had not realised until the sunlight came how small our boat really was…. There was some influence in the light and warmth, some hint of happier days, that made us revive memories of other voyages, when we had stout decks beneath our feet, unlimited food at our command and pleasant cabins for our use. Now we clung to a battered little boat … so low in the water were we that each succeeding swell cut off our view of the sky-line. We were a tiny speck in the vast vista of the sea—the ocean that is … pitiless always to weakness. For a moment the consciousness of the forces arrayed against us would be overwhelming. Then hope and confidence would rise again as our boat rose to a wave and tossed aside the crest in a sparkling shower like the play of prismatic colours at the foot of a waterfall."

Much of the way they were followed by an albatross who, in Shackleton's words, "watched with hard, bright eyes, and seemed to have a quite impersonal interest in our struggle to keep afloat amid the battering seas." They had a shotgun with them in the boat and could have killed the albatross for food, but resisted, thinking of the grim fortunes of the Ancient Mariner. Worsley remarked on the albatross: "… his poetic motion fascinated us, the ease with which he swept the miles aside filled us with envy. He could, with a southwest gale, have made our whole journey in ten hours."

In the daytime, establishing their exact position was a tremendous trial. "Shooting the sun"—that is to say, lining up the sun and the horizon with the sextant to fix a position—was a multi-man effort, especially on a boat, in Worsley's words, "jumping like a flea, shipping seas fore and aft." He described the procedure as follows. "I peered out from our burrow—precious sextant cuddled under my chest to prevent seas falling on it. Sir Ernest stood by under the canvas with chronometer pencil and book. I shouted, 'Stand by,' and knelt on the thwart—two men holding me up on either side. I brought the sun down to where the horizon ought to be and as the boat leaped frantically upward on the crest of a wave, snapped a good guess at the altitude and yelled, 'Stop,' Sir Ernest took the time, and I worked out the result."

It was a rare procedure. The weather was such that in fourteen days Worsley was to take only four sightings of the sun.

At night, on the few occasions they could spot the star, they steered by Antares, known as the Scorpion's Red Eye. Once or twice in the darkness a match from their small supply was lit so the compass reading could be checked.

BATTLE OF JUTLAND

May, 1916
• The German and British fleets meet for the first major naval battle of World War I, in the North Sea waters off Denmark's Jutland Peninsula in May 1916. The Battle of Jutland costs thousands of lives. Each side also loses a battleship many smaller warships.

Shooting the Sun

The sextant, an optical instrument for measuring angular distances, was invented by John Hadley in 1731. Before the arrival of electronic aids to navigation, a familiar sight at sea was a ship's officer on the bridge "shooting the sun" at noon, measuring the altitude of the sun above the horizon in order to determine the ship's latitude.

Worsley referred to their navigation as a "merry game of guesswork"—a wry comment indeed since every mile they sailed off course could result in missing South Georgia altogether.

On the twelfth day the *Caird* went through an extraordinary experience. Shackleton was at the steering device, a makeshift tiller that McNeish had devised. "I called to the other men that the sky was clearing, and then, a moment later, I realised that what I had seen was not a rift in the clouds but the white crest of an enormous wave. During twenty-six years' experience of the ocean in all its moods I had not encountered a wave so gigantic. It was a mighty upheaval of the ocean, a thing quite apart from the big white-capped seas that had been our tireless enemies for many days. I shouted 'For God's sake, hold on! It's got us!' ... White surged the foam of the breaking sea around us. We felt our boat lifted and flung forward like a cork in breaking surf. We were in a seething chaos of tortured water, sagging to the dead weight and shuddering with the blow. We bailed with the energy of men fighting for life, flinging the water over the sides with every receptacle that came to our hands, and after ten minutes of uncertainty we felt the boat renew her life beneath us.

"She floated again and ceased to lurch drunkenly as though dazed by the attack of the sea."

Worsley thought that the wave had been caused by a vast calving of a glacier, a tall cliff of ice toppling into the sea.

Finally, in the early afternoon of May 8, their fifteenth day since leaving Elephant Island there were signs of land ... a drift of seaweed, kelp, and finally the quick wing-flaps of a shag or cormorant, which meant they were fifteen miles or so from the crags of the shore. Even the welcome sight of land, which Worsley reckoned to be Cape Demidov, at the entrance of King Haakon Bay, was tempered by a gale of hurricane-force winds that blew up and forced them to spend an extra day in a cross-sea that tossed up waves forty feet high. Worsley said that none of them had seen anything like it and that the conditions "seemed to have been loosed from the infernal region." Moreover, salt was discovered in the water casks, which meant, as Shackleton put it, "thirst took possession of us." They drank the blubber oil that was on board for emergency use to flatten the seas. The only choice

ROGUE WAVES

Storm waves breaking over the bow of the *Explorer*.

Some years ago I visited the bridge of the *Queen Elizabeth II*. The conversation swung around to waves, rogue waves, that suddenly hump up for no apparent reason and take off like a moving ridge across the seas—much like the one that so startled Shackleton. The captain said his ship had sailed bow first into one such wave, spray from its crest slapping up in sheets against the bridge windows some twelve stories above the water, over one hundred feet. But what had truly been awesome about the wave's size was that it showed up on the ship's radar, reported by a radar officer ... something was coming, a line on his screen, and he wasn't quite sure what it was.

Shackleton had was to land, due to the weakened condition of the boat, and the prevailing winds and current, which were not favorable, the long trip around South Georgia to the whaling stations on the lee shore was out of the question.

Heaving helplessly in the backwash of the heavy seas breaking against the shoreline's cliffs, Shackleton wrote that he had the feeling the end was near. What he had in mind was not the end of the voyage, but of their lives. On the dawn of May 10, in waters that had calmed, they finally decided to make a break for it. They steered the *Caird* toward King Haakon Bay, through a cut in a line of reefs ("like blackened teeth" is Shackleton's description) so narrow that they had to ship their oars to get through.

They landed on a beach where there was shelter under an overhang, and, best of all, a small trickling spring, probably from a glacier, where water was available. The memory of the great wave in mid-voyage continued to haunt Shackleton. In the midst of a fitful sleep he started up and looking out of the cave's entrance, cried out, "Look out, boys, look out! Hold on!...Look! It's just about to break on us."

What he was pointing at was the black wall of a cliff opposite, white-crested with snow, which he mistakenly imagined to be the great sea that had broken over them.

Wandering albatross were nesting in the steep hills above the bay. Back on land, they had no compunctions about killing the young albatrosses for food.

King Haakon Bay
Here in King Haakon Bay, the men of the *James Caird* finally were able to land, first at a small cove and later at a wide beach crowded with elephant seals.

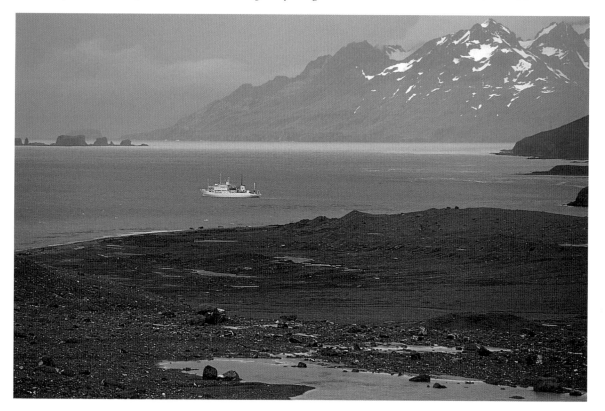

"The flesh was white and succulent and the bones, not fully formed, almost melted in our mouths," Shackleton wrote. "That was a memorable meal."

✧ ✧ ✧

JOURNAL ENTRY, 2002 • *Aboard the* Explorer: *The Scotia Sea*
At the dinner table we got to talking about long open boat journeys. Shackleton's at eight hundred miles in those tumultuous seas was impressive enough, but somebody mentioned that Captain Bligh of the *Bounty* traveled four thousand miles in an open boat after the mutiny. I knew about one voyage five hundred miles longer (more or less down the Pacific Coast of South America) because it involved a very distant relative of mine, Owen Coffin. He was aboard the *Essex* when it was stoved by a whale on the Equator, a thousand miles west of the Galapagos. His grandfather was Hezekiah Coffin, who is said to have been the first to throw tea into Boston Harbor. Owen, who was sixteen when he left Nantucket, has a singular, if somewhat less distinguished, history. He was eaten by his shipmates.

The family story is that starving in mid-ocean, lots were drawn in the small boat to see who would be next, and he drew the short straw. The captain, Pollard by name, offered to take his place, but Coffin refused and put his head over the side so the bullet wouldn't go through the bottom of the boat.

Captain Pollard settled down eventually in Nantucket, a night watchman on the waterfront. Herman Melville, inspired by the *Essex* story to write *Moby Dick*, mentions him in his poem "Clarel": *A night patrolman on the quay / Watching the bales till morning hour.*

On one occasion Capt. Pollard was asked if by chance he knew Owen Coffin. "Know him," Pollard was reported to have answered. "Why, I *et* him!"

✧ ✧ ✧

The situation that now faced them was that having come fifteen hundred miles they had only about twenty-two miles to go (at least as the crow flies) to reach the sanctuary of a whaling station. What they had to cross was utterly unknown territory—a forbidding stretch of mountains and glaciers. The chart they had in their possession showed only the outlines of the coast. The interior was blank; it could just as well have indicated a desert. The voyage from Elephant Island had taken such a toll on the group that Shackleton decided they should rest for four days before attempting the climb.

Whaler
A portrait thought to be of Owen Chase, also aboard the *Essex*. A successful whaling captain, late in life he began hiding food in the attic of his home on Orange Street, Nantucket. Judged insane, he died in 1869. Captain George Pollard went to sea again in a ship called *The Two Brothers*. Attached to the ceiling of his cabin he kept a net filled with vegetables and fruit so that all he had to do to eat was reach up. That ship was wrecked as well—not by a whale but in reefs southwest of Hawaii.

Once they regained strength, the first stage of the journey was once again in the *Caird*, to the head of the bay, where they could see a pass up into the mountains. It took them four hours to pull ashore on a sandy beach that teemed with elephant seals. They dragged the *Caird* up above the high water mark, turned it over, and made a temporary home that Shackleton named Peggotty Camp, after the Dickens character who lived in a hut made out of a boat. One curious aspect of this scene was an acre or so of ships' wreckage—broken oars, masts, even part of a figurehead. One of the touching bits of flotsam was a little model of a ship's hull, apparently a child's toy. In the moonlight of their first night in their new shelter, Crean reported he'd seen a rat—very likely, he thought, one that had come in with the wreckage.

Thus they slept under the *James Caird*, much as their companions were doing back on Elephant Island. One of them, Vincent, was never truly able to recover, and lay apathetically in his sleeping bag. Shackleton decided to leave him at King Haakon Bay with McCarthy, who had come out of the ordeal the strongest of the men, putting McNeish in nominal command. He picked Crean and Worsley to go with him.

They stayed on the beach for three days, waiting for the weather to clear, Shackleton increasingly restless—concerned about his men on Elephant Island as well as those of his little group. The winter season was fast approaching, minimizing the chances of budging from where they were.

Shelter
The overhang of a cliff provided shelter for the men of the *James Caird* on their first night ashore. As McNeish remembered, "...the Boss found a cave & drove us into it for the night."

Crossing the
Mountains
MAY 19–20, 1916

At 2 A.M. on a calm moonlit night, Shackleton, Crean, and Worsley started off from King Haakon Bay. The only one with any experience in the mountains was Worsley, who had climbed in New Zealand and the Alps. With them they had three days' supply of food packed in a sock for each man, a Primus stove filled with enough oil to cook six hot meals, a pot, matches, two compasses, a pair of binoculars, a length of rope, and Worsley's chronometer, which he carried hanging from his neck. McNeish had fitted the heels of Shackleton's boots with screws he'd taken from the *James Caird* to give him a better purchase on the snow and ice. They brought along staves of wood from the *Caird*'s decking to use as walking sticks, as well as McNeish's carpenter's adze to use as an ice axe. That was all they had. They left their sleeping bags behind, which meant that the traverse would have to be completed without any prolonged rest.

Almost as soon as they started climbing for the interior a fog drifted into the mountains from the sea, so thick that they were forced to tether each to the other with a rope. Worsley, as the navigator and the last man in line, would call out "port," "starboard," and "steady" to keep Shackleton, breaking the trail in front, on the right course. For rest, every fifteen minutes or so each would fall backward, arms outstretched in the snow.

Finally, the fog cleared in the early morning and they reached a point where they could look down on Possession Bay. They had crossed the island at its narrowest, but the mountains

REPEAT PERFORMANCES

A 1920's photograph of the *James Caird* on exhibit outside London's Royal Albert Hall, where Shackleton was lecturing. The boat was too large to be set up inside.

Two expeditions have tried to replicate the voyage of the *James Caird* and the traverse of South Georgia. In 1993, four men and a woman got into a facsimile of the *Caird* called *Sir Ernest Shackleton* and sailed off from Elephant Island. Although they landed safely in South Georgia, they never attempted to cross the mountains, and became rather a burden, it turned out, on the local British authorities because they ran out of funds with no means or the wherewithal to get off the island. In 1997, a seven-man Irish crew sailed on a replica called *Tom Crean*. In a kind of weird testimonial to Shackleton's accomplishments, the newcomers came a cropper; their boat capsized frequently in the heavy seas, and finally had to be abandoned and scuttled halfway across.

There have also been attempts to follow the South Georgia crossing. Frank Hurley, who was compiling his photographs for a book on the expedition, though far better outfitted for the traverse, found it impossible, even in perfect weather. In recent times, Conrad Anker (who in 1999 discovered the body of George Mallory on Mount Everest, where it had lain at 27,000 feet since 1924), Reinhold Messner, the first to climb Everest without oxygen, and Stephen Venables managed in three days to complete the trip Shackleton had made in less than two. Perhaps the weirdest moment on that cross-island trek was the sight at about the halfway point of what at first they took to be a "glacier erratic" boulder. As they drew closer it turned out to be the twisted hulk of a Wessex helicopter that had crashed during the Falklands War. Nose down, it is slowly disappearing into the ice, as if wishing to continue its journey downward, leaving behind to this day (so they reported) the faintest odor of hydraulic fluid.

dropped abruptly into the bay with no shelter or beaches at their base. They were forced to backtrack. All that day they were brought up short by impassable ridges and false leads.

Eventually their way was barred by a line of five craggy peaks, almost like the blunt fingers of an enormous hand against the sky. They tried the first two passes between the peaks and each time had to retrace their steps. "Each of the climbs were steeper," Worsley wrote, "and the third one, which brought us to about five thousand feet above sea level, was very exhausting."

By this time they had been on their climb for a numbing thirteen hours. The urge to rest must have been compelling as they retraced their steps and climbed again into the final, most northern of the four passages between the five peaks. Here they looked over a precipice that dropped down three hundred feet onto a long snow slope that disappeared into the mist.

Shackleton surveyed the situation at some length and finally said, "We've got to take a risk. Are you game?"

They began the descent of the cliff, inching their way down, Shackleton cutting footholes with McNeish's adze, until finally the three men were standing at the top of a snow slope. With darkness coming on, the three had no idea whether it leveled out far below, or whether a few yards out it dropped precipitously, a cliff edge.

Worsley reported later that Shackleton had said, "It's a devil of a risk, but we've got to take it. We'll slide."

The three arranged themselves as if on an imaginary toboggan, each straddled behind the other.

They pushed off.

It is one of the few moments in the saga of the *Endurance* that brings a smile to the face—the image of the three of them as if on a sled, a typical winter scene that one equates with Christmas revelry on the hill up beyond the barn, and yet in this case in a wintery fastness where no man had ever set foot before. The three were suddenly gripped by childhood memories: "We seemed to shoot into space. For a moment my hair fairly stood on end. Then quite suddenly I was grinning! I was actually enjoying it.... I yelled with excitement, and found that Shackleton and Crean were yelling too."

At the end of their ride, leveling off and gently stopped by a bank of snow, they stood up, dusted themselves off, and shook hands.

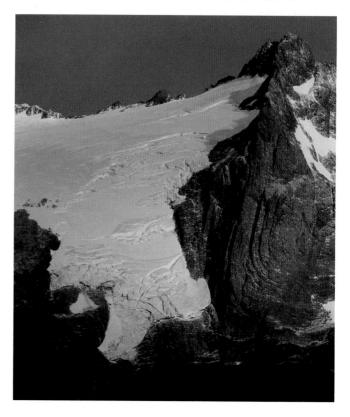

Stromness
The glacial terrain above Stromness Bay suggests the difficulties facing Shackleton, Worsley, and Crean as they came near the end of their trek.

THE FOURTH MAN

"The following lines were stimulated by the account of one of the Antarctic expeditions," wrote T.S. Eliot.

One of mysteries of Shackleton's climb is that each of the three had the feeling that someone else was with them, a fourth man, and what was especially eerie was that each of the men came to this notion quite independently, admitting it to each other some weeks after their climb. Much was made of this, illustrations in weeklies, showing a dim white figure trudging along with the others. Some compared it to the vision of the Angel of Mons, a woman on a white horse carrying a flaming sword rumored to have appeared to the British troops on the battlefields of the Western Front. T. S. Eliot makes use of the image in the *Waste Land*:

> Who is the third who walks always beside you?
> When I count, there are only you and I
> together
> But when I look up the white road
> There is always another one walking beside you
> Gliding wrapt in a brown mantle, hooded
> I do not know whether a man or a woman
> — But who is that on the other side of you?

It was not, however, the end of their difficulties. Darkness had fallen. Frustrated by one false lead after another they pushed on past midnight. Shackleton, who had kept to a strict schedule of one minute's rest every quarter hour, decided a longer stop was necessary. Crean and Worsley fell to the snow and huddled against each for warmth instantly fell asleep. Typical of Shackleton's strength of will, he stayed awake, and after five minutes roused the two and persuaded them that they had been asleep for half an hour. He later wrote, "I realized it would be disastrous if we all slumbered, for sleep under such conditions merges into death."

Once again they set out to try to find a passage across a ridge that still blocked a descent to the coast. As the second dawn of their travail broke over the mountains they reached a gap from where with mounting excitement they could recognize the rock formations around Stromness. For the second time they shook hands. As Crean prepared a celebratory hot breakfast cooked on the Primus stove with the last of their fuel, Shackleton climbed along the ridge to get a better view. It was 6:30 A.M. In the distance from the direction of Stromness he thought he heard a faint steam whistle and knew from his stay at Grytviken that it was the signal for the men at the whaling stations to rouse themselves for the day's work. He clambered down to the others to tell them what he'd heard and that at seven sharp the whistle would sound again to signal the start of the workday.

One can imagine the excitement as they crouched around Worsley's chronometer and watched the second hand tick toward the hour mark. At precisely seven the faint wail of the steam whistle reached them, the first sound they heard from humankind other than their own since December 14, 1914. They looked at each other. Worsley yelled out the first thing that came to mind. "Yoicks!" he shouted. "Tally-Ho!"

JOURNAL ENTRY, 2002 • *Fortuna Bay, South Georgia*
The sea is flat and calm. We went ashore in the Zodiacs to take what on shipboard has been referred to as the Shackleton Walk—in fact the last two miles or so of his

extraordinary trek across South Georgia Island. We started up from the beach at Fortuna Bay around the corner from Stromness station to intercept Shackleton's route just as it drops down into off the Crean glacier into a boggy meadow that stretches to Cumberland Bay, Stromness itself a short jaunt to the right.

We hooked around a high rock outcropping and I started up a ravine, grasping handfuls of tussock grass to haul myself up. It is not easy. The ship's doctor (he was accompanied by his wife and two young daughters, who moved from rock to rock like klipspringers) hung around above me to see if I needed a hand. He's a good man to have looking after me: Doctor John, as everyone calls him, is well over six feet, once played for the Seattle Seahawks.

About two hundred yards up the climb, I lost my footing and fell in a hole amid the tussock, wedged in there quite nicely, not really minding because it gave me a chance to take a breather and to look out over the restless sea far below. Just then, off to one side, the tussock grass bent alarmingly. I looked over to see a fur seal advancing at a considerable clip through the tussock, quite obviously bent on mischief.

My first impulse, of course, was to reach for the stones to clap them together, but being stuck in the hole, it was another matter. I might have been able to get one stone out, but then, as I wondered about it subsequently, what is the sound of one stone clapping?

Fur Seals

My nemesis, the fur seal, is one of the "eared" seals, along with sea lions and walruses. Unlike "true" seals, which are largely aquatic animals and must undulate awkwardly over the ground to get anywhere, the "eared" seals can be found high up in the tussock, snouts turned up in lordly disdain, able to rear up on their flippers, rotate their hinds legs and sprint for a short distance at quite a clip.

So I resorted to shouting loudly, clapping my mittens together—a rapid, if somewhat muted pillowy sound, as the seal hurried toward me through the tussock on the elbows of his flippers.

His mouth was ajar; I had a glimpse of the back of his throat, a pair of yellowed tusks (he was not more than ten feet away), and then for reasons of his own, perhaps the shouting, perhaps the flapping of mittens in his face, he chose to stop, and indeed withdraw—an apparition gone in the tussock.

In my curious career I have been charged a number of times—elephant, gorilla, rhino (demonstration charges, thank goodness, just to let me know I was encroaching), out-of-control skiers, skateboarders, errant bicyclists, football linebackers—and on one occasion, stepping out of the basket of a hot-air balloon I was charged by an angry bull in a Florida field. But my experience with the fur seal, trapped, utterly unable to move, is at the top of the list.

The doctor appeared, looming over a tussock. My intuitive reaction was to flap my mittens at him, fur seals still on my mind.

"It's you," I said inanely.

He put out a hand and I pulled myself out of the tussock hole.

✧ ✧ ✧

At Stromness station the first human beings to see them were two boys who took one startled look and fled. As they came through town, the station foreman, a man named Matthias Andersen, thought for an instant that they were three whalers recovering from a severe alcoholic binge. Worsley wore three large safety pins to keep his clothes from falling off—a circus clown outfit, and indeed when Andersen went to the manager's house he explained to the station manager that waiting outside the door were three "funny-looking men."

Upon this, the manager used an expressive Norwegian phrase of skepticism: "One has to hear much before one's ears fall off."

But he went to the door.

Shackleton reports the following exchange:

" 'Well?'

" 'Don't you know me?'

" 'I know your voice,' he replied doubtfully. 'You're the mate of the *Daisy*.'

" 'My name is Shackleton,' I said.

"Immediately he put out his hand and said, 'Come in. Come in.'

Ghost Towns

One by one the windtorn whaling communities are literally disappearing. The weather has started the decay; an occasional demolition crew—I met one of them hitching a ride on *Explorer*—is completing the work. Even Stromness, perhaps the most famous for being where Shackleton came back to civilization (the manager's house is above) is doomed

Gentoos

The *Explorer* near Stromness, at a colony of gentoo penguins. The gentoo, distinguished by a white patch over its eye, is a *Pygoscelid* penguin, which loosely translated means "rump-legged"—an apt description of the waddle over the ice that one associates with all penguins.

Seal Haven

The fur seals have an easier time getting in and out of the deserted buildings of the whaling stations. These are elephant seals, which can weigh up to four tons. Unlikely, but perhaps one of them caused the hole in the floor.

" 'Tell me, when was the war over?' I asked.

" 'The war is not over,' he answered, 'Millions are being killed. Europe is mad. The world is mad.' "

According to Worsley's account, Shackleton then said, "I'm afraid we smell."

"That doesn't matter," replied the manager. "We're used to it on a whaling station."

✧ ✧ ✧

JOURNAL ENTRY, 2002 • *Stromness and Grytviken*

As we came down a ravine and started across a boggy meadow toward Stromness, the thought crossed my mind that had the two boys from Shackleton's time, eighty-six years before, spotted our group approaching Stromness from the interior, they would have been equally startled ... surely the sight of our bright red parkas alone would have sent them scurrying, wide-eyed, back to report that an alien red-backed tribal people was emerging from the mountains.

Stromness had been deserted for years. On the beach we walked past a number of propellers, tall as a man, which must have once powered the whale factory ships. In town, the massive sheds are torn and fragile, thin sheets of rust-colored metal shifting in the wind, the hulks of the oversize machinery used to "render" the whales lying about everywhere, everything

covered in a curious, orange-y hue of decay. The seals and penguins have taken over, and it is possible, though I didn't see it myself, to catch sight of one looking out a window or standing in a doorway.

We went to look at the manager's house. White facade. The bathtub is upstairs, indeed the one that Shackleton slipped wearily into, and gratefully, after his descent off the mountain ridge. None of the three had changed clothes or had a bath for over two years.

We had been warned not to go into any of the buildings—too rickety. Nonetheless, my friend Bob, quite like him, went back in there among the ruins, disappearing through an open door to look around. Gloomy. Light barely filtering through. No sign of penguins. Or seals. He told me this later. It would have been nice to see Bob creep up behind a seal looking out a window and peer over his shoulder. No such luck.

We boarded *Explorer* and eased up the coast into the natural harbor of Cumberland Bay with Grytviken at its head. In 1967, when whaling was closed down by international decree, the sixteen stations on South Georgia were completely abandoned, as if those who worked there—as many as three hundred men—had been suddenly stricken by the plague or frightened off the properties by some hideous rumor of something on the way.

Grytviken was one the largest whaling stations. A couple who act as caretakers live on a small yacht tied up at the quay. We went ashore. The church at Grytviken has been restored. Next to it is a "kino" (cinema)

Whalers' Church

The Norwegian-style church in which Shackleton's funeral was held. Quite functional, it was restored as a project after the Falklands' War by British troops stationed at nearby King Edward Point garrison. Inside the church are memorials to Shackleton and to Carl Anton Larsen, an explorer and whaler who arrived in 1904 with a fleet of whaling ships. In thirty-four seasons Larsen was said to have harpooned 6,000 whales. He too had been shipwrecked—in 1903 spending a winter with his men on Paulet Island, at the mouth of the Weddell Sea, amidst an Adélie penguin colony whose occupants provided sustenance for all.

where films were shown—always with considerable audience participation—catcalls, heavy moaning during the love scenes, and so forth. According to the guide, there was a ski run behind the church, as well as a soccer field, but no pitch for cricket, which was apparently not a whalers' game. What is not evident on our visit, of course, and the curse of the whaling stations, was the hideous smell. Pastor Loken of the church wrote of it: "The smell was everywhere after the first whale was caught. It was in our food, in our coffee, in the water with which we washed, in our clothes, and in our bunks. We were steeped in it."

We visited the little graveyard. Some of the stones are marked 1912, the year a ship brought typhus to nearby Grytviken and a dozen whalers died.

The Explorer's Grave

The procession from the Whaler's Church with Shackleton's coffin was preceded by two men carrying black funeral banners, an early symbolic tradition to ward off evil spirits. Here under this simple grave, they laid the explorer to rest.

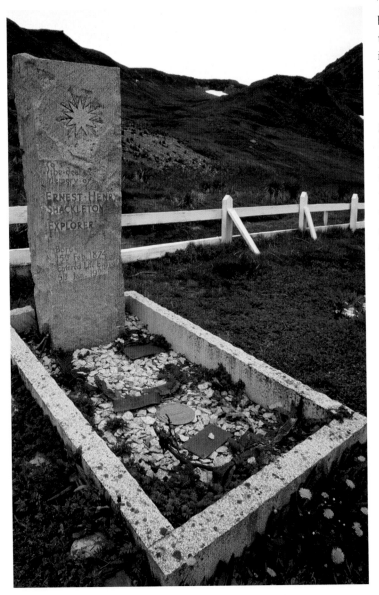

The stones lie flat, sometimes with a border of pebbles. Dandelions are said to grow here and there, the seeds imported from Norway and planted to make the incumbents feel more at home, but I didn't see any.

At the back is Shackleton's gravestone, a tall upright structure marked on the front with a nine-pointed star, a symbol he used as part of his coat of arms. On the back of the stone is a Robert Browning quotation: "I hold that a man should strive to the uttermost for his life's set prize."

During the Falklands War, an Argentine submarine, the *Sante Fe*, was forced to the surface by British naval forces and brought alongside the quay at Grytviken. Its crew came on deck, hands up, standing in a row, when one of them suddenly disappeared back into a hatch. He was shot when he came out, killed, though apparently he'd gone below simply to fetch his kit. The English thought he might be popping back out with a grenade perhaps, or a submachine gun, so he was gunned down. His name was Felix Artuso, and he is buried in the little graveyard under a simple cross—the only upright marker at the site other than Shackleton's.

JOURNAL ENTRY, 2002 • *Gold Harbor*

We saw the South Georgia pipit, a target bird! Two of them, one flying off and dropping abruptly into a barish patch in the tussock, to be followed by the other, as if the two were playing hide-and-seek. I am not really a great pipit fan. They are brown-streaked ground birds, thin-billed, with a habit of bobbing their tails. They tend to walk rather than hop, which is a nice characteristic, but I wasn't close enough to check this out. I thought, I've come twelve thousand miles to see this bird, so I kept my binoculars on the pair until they followed each other over a ridge. I thought, well, now, the next time the general conversation in a living room full of birding people turns to pipits, I can call out "Ahem," and drop the South Georgia pipit on them. It'll just be a question of getting them talking about pipits so that I can do this, not an easy matter.

After the pipit sighting, Trip, who is the lead tour-leader, took me up on a high ridge to look at the wandering albatross in their nesting area. It was a long haul, at least for me, but well worth the effort. It is the largest of the albatross, eleven-foot wing span. The birds nest apart in the high ridges—solitary figures in the tussock. They have no fear of humans. We sat for a long time and watched one on its nest. They lay a single large egg and the incubation period is long, two months, and the young chicks get parental care for almost a year. The wind, a constant steady force, sighed through the tussock and ruffled the bird's feathers. The bird made a gentle clacking sound with its bill, which is large, hooked, imperious, and startlingly pink. We moved away to sit and watch a pair engaged in a mating dance, long wings outstretched, and what it made it quite comical was that underneath them and constantly getting in the way was a fur seal pup. The birds stumbled over it, and the seal, obviously trying to get out of the way, only seemed to move to wherever the birds chose to step in their dance, as if his presence, being trod underfoot, was somehow part of the ritual.

At one point, the other albatross sitting on their nests off on their distant hills raised their wings as one—a kind of symbiotic salute, it seemed, in recognition of the relationship between the two … however messed up they were with the seal underfoot.

Songbird Survivor

One of the mysteries about the South Georgia pipit is how it survives the severe winters. All the other birds—the skuas, the cormorants, the albatross, kelp gulls, all those with marine life habits—move out. It would take a hardy ornithologist indeed to spend a winter finding out how the pipit does it. Most likely the bird feeds on dried seeds, seaweed, lichens, perhaps even carrion if desperate enough.

Elephant Island

APRIL–OCTOBER 1916

The mood of those watching the *James Caird* disappear into the mist was mixed. Wild, now in charge, who had led the group in sending them off with three hearty cheers, overheard one of them remarking, "That's the last of them." "I almost knocked him down with a rock, but satisfied myself by addressing a few remarks to him in real lower deck language."

The first order of business was to provide shelter for the twenty-two men left behind after the *Caird*'s departure. What was eventually referred to as the Snuggery was constructed by overturning the two cutters, *Stancomb-Wills* and *Dudley Docker*, putting them side by side and setting up living quarters within. A large tent covered the entire structure. The chimney of the bogie, or stove, was made out of the lining of a biscuit tin stuck up through the bottom of the uppermost boat. A funnel-like door, a kind of sleeve, served as the entrance. Later, small windowpanes, made of celluloid, were cut out of the boat's sides. Down the way an oar served as a flagpole, from it fluttering—a perky touch—the burgee of the Royal Thames Yacht Club, under whose name the *Endurance* had been registered.

Wild dictated the sleeping arrangements—ten men (including all the foc's'le hands) in the top "bunks" and the rest arranged on the "floor"...resembling, Hurley wrote, "mummies in a catacomb." It was impossible to stand upright. Twenty-two men were crammed into a space that measured about 19 by 10 feet.

FRANK HURLEY

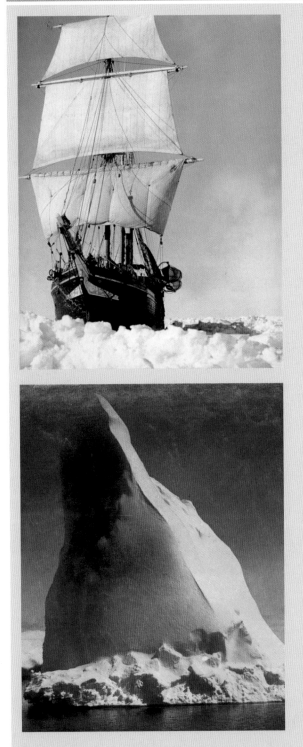

It is doubtful that the *Endurance* saga would hold as much fascination without the pictures and movie footage shot by Frank Hurley. He was born in Sydney on Oct. 15 1885. After an adventurous youth, at the age of 13 he hopped a freight train into the mountains and took a job as an assistant fitter in an ironworks. He returned to Sydney and began technical training courses at night. Fascinated by photography, he wrote in a diary: "From the first time I gazed wondrously at the miracle of chemical reaction or the latent image during the process of development I knew I had found my life's work…"

He went into the postcard business with a friend, his cards distinguished by their dramatic effects— familiar landmarks against romanticized backdrops, often composites, sometimes with hand-coloring to enhance the mood.

The artistic need to improve on the original was typical of him, not only in photography (he was known to embellish photos from the *Endurance* expedition) but in his personal life, which he also tended to romanticize. He liked to say that his recruitment to Shackleton's *Endurance* expedition was made known to him by an Aboriginal runner handing him a cable deep in the Outback. For a brief time he was the official photographer on the Western Front with the New Zealand forces, sent to the Ypres Salient. He got into trouble with his superiors for producing staged photographs in which he would superimpose striking sunsets over the battlefields, rearrange the cannon barrels for better dramatic effect, and so on, very much what he had done in his postcard days. War stilled neither his artistic nor his romantic leanings: In April 1918, with peace still months away, he married a young Anglo-French opera singer after a ten-day courtship.

Considering the incredible hardships endured during the *Endurance* expedition, it is surprising Hurley didn't chuck the whole business. It was as if he stood

On December 21, 1914, Hurley wrote in his diary: "At 10 A.M. we entered long leads of ice-free water in which were drifting some fine bergs of magnificent forms. One, a fine cuniformed mass, 200 feet high, I photographed."

apart from the drama, however desperate, to record it as it unfolded—a good example is that he saved three exposures in his little "Vest Pocket" Kodak camera to take in case Shackleton ever arrived back at Elephant Island to rescue his men. Orde-Lees writes that Hurley never played in the make-up soccer games on the ice, that "he never plays games...busy with his cinema and cameras all the time..."

Hurley often complained in his diary of working his cameras in the sub-zero conditions of the Antarctic. "My camera is a bugbear and using it is a nightmare. Every time I have to set the shutter I have to take a number of tiny screws from the front [with gloves off] and bend the mechanism into shape." Invariably, the chilled screws would stick to his skin—a painful process to take his bare hand away.

Hussey's Banjo
The instrument weighed twelve pounds, which made Hussey worry about whether Shackleton would allow him to keep it.

It reeked, of course, from guano, the more as the floor warmed up and slowly sank into the rookery goo.

On June 15, about two months after Shackleton's departure, Blackborrow was operated on for his frostbitten toes, which had turned gangrenous. The Snuggery was turned into an operating room, stoked up to 79 degrees; what they had for surgical instruments were boiled in a hoosh pot. McIlroy performed the operation, which took fifty-five minutes. The operation was a success. Greenstreet, one of the few witnesses (the rest were sent out to a cave where they sang songs while they waited) remarked, "The poor beggar behaved splendidly." Orde-Lees was upset at the amount of chloroform used for the operation, so little left that he wondered what would happen if *he* had to be operated on.

Not unexpectedly, Wild had problems with Orde-Lees ("the pessimist" as he referred to him), mainly for his recommendation, often expressed with great heat, that a winter's supply of penguins and seals should be collected before they left on migration, an action (very much like Shackleton's opinion at Patience Camp) that Wild felt would discourage the men, that they would realize they were in for the long haul rather than being rescued in a few weeks or so. Wild wrote later: "I had to threaten to shoot him to make him keep his tongue between his teeth."

Poor Orde-Lees. According to Hussey, if the food ran out and cannibalism was the only hope to survive, Orde-Lees was the first choice to eat! His snoring in the confines of the Snuggery bothered his bunkmates to such an extent that a slip noose was attached to his arm which ran through a series of eyelets to the bunks in his vicinity. Those who were awakened by what Hurley refers to as "habitual trumpeting" would haul vigorously on the line. "But Lees is incorrigible, scarcely heeding our signals," Hurley wrote. "It has been suggested that the noose might be tied around his neck."

As the days settled into weeks, and then into months, it was evident that a rescue would not be forthcoming soon, if ever. Greenstreet wrote of life in the Snuggery, "Everyone spent the day rotting in their bags with blubber and tobacco smoke. So passes another goddam rotten day."

Wild did his best to arrange diversions to keep up the men's morale, much of it by insisting on a strict schedule.

The Snuggery
The "Hut" on Elephant Island just after its completion, before the chimney was made and put into place on May 3, 1916. Socks and other clothes are left to dry on the hull.

The camp routine went as follows: The cook was called at 7 A.M. Breakfast (penguin steaks) at 8:45. Those who were not up were roused by Wild calling for everybody to "lash up and stow! The Boss may come today!"—which meant rolling up the sleeping gear and stowing it. At meals, sitting on boxes that had been the support for the cook's bed, the men circled the stove, moving one seat at a time so all shared the warmth equally. At 12:30 a light lunch was served, the afternoon spent at various tasks (mending, snaring, skinning) and then an evening hoosh at 4:30.

One of the entertainments was to reminisce about one's favorite foods. Hurley made a list of them: Macklin wanted many seconds of scrambled eggs on toast; McIlroy, a marmalade pudding and cream; Wild, any old dumpling as long as it was a large one; Greenstreet, one of his mother's Christmas puddings with cream; Marston, macaroni and cheese; James, treacle pudding; Rickenson, blackberry and apple pudding.

Hurley summed it up by noting that the trend of tastes was for sweetstuffs. "I firmly believe each would give all his earnings for his fill."

In the evening the blubber lamp was ignited in the center of the seated circle. Hurley writes, "The light thrown up illuminates smoke coloured faces like stage footlights. The sparkling eyes and glint on the aluminium mugs, the stream of flickering light thrown out from the open bogie door, making weird dancing shadows on the inside of the boats, makes me think of a council of brigands holding revelry after an escape in a chimney or coalmine. I can imagine the look of surprise and bewilderment with which any visitor

Preparing Supper

Skinning seals on Elephant Island. In late August the seals had gone; only two cases of rations remained. Charles Green, the cook, later told James Fisher, a Shackleton biographer, "Earlier in the expedition, if anybody killed a seal, they had the brains for perks. But later on, on Elephant Island, we were starving—it was suggested that we were going to have to cast lots to see which one was going to be done in first. I said to them, 'Whoever is going to be killed, I'm going to have the job of cooking him—and I want the brains…'"

Say Cheese?

Ever the optimist, Hurley wrote, "Sunshine day with gorgeous pink glow on the peaks at sunset. Took photo of group—the most motley and unkempt assemblage that ever was projected on a plate."

BATTLE OF THE SOMME

• War on the Western Front rages during the summer of 1916, as the British and French try to outmaneuver the Germans at the Somme River. With the help of tanks, the Allies gain ground. But the Allies fail to achieve surprise, so the fighting drags on, leading to some of the heaviest casualties of the war.

would regard this grizzly, bearded, and unkempt assemblage could he be suddenly thrown among us. Bewilderment would speedily become aversion, for our blubbery emanations and the odours from 22 crowded, and 'seven months unwasheds' coupled with the blue liquid tobacco smoke 'fog' must be productive of an atmosphere distinctly unsavoury."

After what was called Smoke Oh, the boxes were returned to re-form the bottom of the cook's bunk; those with bunks swung into them with "monkey-like agility," and the rest crawled into their sleeping bags on the floor "like gigantic snails."

Hussey then treated everyone to a half hour's serenade with his banjo, accompanied by those who were still awake in their sleeping bags. Hussey used to say of his banjo that he had charmed cannibals in the Sudan. Hurley, though more circumspect, wrote of it as being "indispensable despite a limited repertoire." To the strumming of the banjo, they made up songs about each other, and if there objections to the target of the gibes, a worse one was sure to follow the following week. Reginald James wrote a ballad about Frank Wild, much surprising his shipmates because he was considered a rather dry academic sort, which went as follows: *My name is Franky Wild-o and my hut's on Elephant Isle. | The wall's without a single brick and the roof's without a tile. | Yet, nevertheless, you must confess by many and many a mile. | It's the most palatial dwelling place you'll find on Elephant Isle.*

Outside the Snuggery the weather was foul by any standard. The blizzards blew ice sheets around the site that were the size of window panes. On the 15 of July the side of a nearby glacier collapsed into the bay and if it had not

been for loose brash ice smothering and diminishing the huge wave that was kicked up, its wash would have swept over Camp Wild.

Hurley, of course, noted the few pleasant days with splendid enthusiasm: "The most wondrous display of colour my eye has ever witnessed transported the glacier into a riot of tints fantastic and unreal...if you see Venice you may die, but witness these glories of nature and you will feel it is much better to live."

Hurley's was very much a minority view. After four months the food began to run out. Men were sent out to scrape limpets off the rocks. Orde-Lees, who had prophesied this might happen, noted such mocking remarks as "We shall have to eat the one who dies first" and mourned that "there's many a true word said in jest."

✧ ✧ ✧

Journal Entry, 2002 • *Elephant Island*

An hour off Elephant Island, we were lucky enough to spot two humpback whales, one of them breaching, half turning in an arc as it came out of the sea. Both whales came close aboard, a deep turquoise blue as their shadows moved alongside the ship.

The occasional cruise ship often sits a mile off Elephant Island, unable to unload in passengers in the Zodiacs. But for us it is reasonably calm now, and the captain tells us we should be able to land and inspect the saddle on Elephant Island where Shackleton settled his men while he set off for South Georgia. Long, bouncy trip around to the lee shore.

Going ashore, the procedure is to arrange oneself on the rounded side of the Zodiac with one's back to the shore and then swing one's legs over the side and step down, hoping the surge will retreat enough so that you feel solid sand or stones underfoot.

So what do I do going ashore on Elephant Island but step over the side of the Zodiac just as it lifted on an incoming surge, and the water poured into the top of one of my yellow boots. I hoped that the warmth of my foot would thaw out the moisture, but not at all. I squished about all afternoon. It occurred to me how inconsequential this was compared to the daily torment Shackleton's crowd went through every day.

Very rocky, hard to stroll around. So I sat on a rock and contemplated. The usual fur seals, and one large female elephant seal. Obviously the island is named after the elephant seals, but there were none recorded during the stay of the *Endurance* people.

Skua

The skua is a large (three pounds) gull-like brown bird with hawk-like instincts. It has the distinction of being the world's most southerly bird: the species has been recorded at the South Pole. They are the nemesis of penguin colonies, taking chicks or eggs at will. Also they practice what is called kleptoparisitics, the ability to harass seabirds to drop or regurgitate their prey, often retrieving it for themselves before it reaches the water.

Birds pretty much limited to cape petrel, giant petrel, skuas, sheathbills. The sheathbill's feet aren't webbed like the seabirds. It's white-colored and looks like a hen wandering among the rocks. The chinstrap penguins slide down the sheen of the rocks, teetering, like teenagers on a diving board as they wait for the right surge before slipping into the sea.

Out there are the leopard seals—the penguins' nemesis. Up to six feet in length, they are well named for their coloration. But the leopard seal's head is oddly reptilian, the face of an anaconda. They have a gruesome way of preparing a penguin for consumption, namely by shaking it loose from its skin, snapping it violently against the surface of the sea so that the bird is turned inside out. The discarded skins often float onshore. (We've seen them, the head usually attached, a grim reminder of its end.)

My shipmates are beginning to gather at the shore's edge to wait for the Zodiacs to fetch them. There is not much to see or do at Cape Wild except wander about and wonder what it must have been like. Back from the beach there is a tall cross with a plaque at its base that commemorates not Shackleton but the Chileans whose tugboat *Yelcho* retrieved the Elephant Island contingent. The captain's likeness is on a Chilean stamp, and the prow of the *Yelcho* is preserved in a cradle in a supermarket parking lot in Puerto Williams, a Chilean naval community on the Beagle Channel.

I can see the Zodiacs are beginning to load up. When we reach the ship and climb up the steeply banked gangplank to enter at midships, we are required to slide a wooden counter across a bulletin board to signify we are on board. The stewards are waiting with mugs of hot cocoa to take off the chill. If all the counters are not pulled across, up on the bridge the binoculars come out and the ship's officers look shoreward for a poppy-red parka among the

Humpback's Tail

Those aboard a Zodiac enjoy one of the great sights of the Antarctic, though hardly as common as it once was. Captain Larsen of the sealing ship *Jason* in 1892 wrote that "countless schools of blue whales, as many as twenty at a time, and several hundred fin and humpback whales would swim right up to the ship's side." From South Georgia alone from 1904 to 1965 when the whaling industry closed down, the take of blue whales was 41,515. The largest, it is now also the rarest of the whales.

rocks of someone perhaps deep in thought who has lost track of time and has been left behind. It hasn't happened yet, much less in a spot as desolate and bleak as Cape Wild on Elephant Island.

◇ ◇ ◇

When Shackleton reached South Georgia, rescue missions were obviously in mind, two of them in fact, first to get the three men from Peggotty Camp in King Haakon Bay at the other side of the island, and then to fetch the *Endurance* contingent off Elephant Island. A whale-catcher named *Samson* was sent for McNeish, McCarthy, and Vincent. Worsley was on board. When the *Samson* pulled into King Haakon Bay, McCarthy expressed his disappointment that Worsley, his captain, hadn't been part of the rescue group. In Worsley's words, " 'Well, I'm here,' and they stared... They had been in my presence daily for [almost] two years, but failed to recognize me after a bath, a shave, and a change of clothing."

Worsley had the *James Caird* hauled aboard the *Samson* and brought it back with him. When they arrived at Stromness, the Norwegians as a man went down to the wharf to touch the whale boat and claim the honor of bringing her to shore. Worsley remembered, "I think Shackleton must have felt it was one of his proudest moments. The [gesture] was so spontaneous... that it was quite affecting."

Worsley describes a reception for Shackleton and his companions at which various old-timers came forward to express their admiration at what they had done. One included in his remarks (which were translated from the Norwegian) that he knew the stormy "Southern Ocean" intimately and that bringing a twenty-foot boat 800 miles across such an ocean and then capping that by climbing across the snow and ice of the interior of South Georgia was something he could hardly imagine. He concluded his remarks by exclaiming, "These are men!"

Arrangements were made for Shackleton to return to Elephant Island. Only three day after arriving, he left Stromness on a steam whaler named the *Southern Sky.* One hundred miles from Elephant Island she ran into pack ice and was only able to push forty miles further before being brought up fast. It was decided to return not to South Georgia but to the Falkland Islands to look for a more suitable rescue ship and to cable home news of their situation.

There had been no word of Shackleton or his whereabouts for fifteen months. In Europe the news shared the headlines with accounts of the Battle of Jutland—the last great fleet action of the battlewagons of World War I. Even the German papers published the news. While there was considerable excitement amongst the general public, a kind of lift from the bad war news, Shackleton's cabled attempts to get help from the Admiralty were

Skeptic

When Winston Churchill (here shown as commander of the 6th Battalion, Royal Scots Fusiliers) heard of Shackleton's failed expedition, he wrote his wife from the carnage of the Ypres Salient in 1916, "Fancy that ridiculous Shackleton & his South Pole—in the crash of the world." Both men were born the same year, but Churchill outlived Shackleton by close to half a century.

unsuccessful. Indeed, the Admiralty was scornful that Shackleton should suppose warships could be used to rescue marooned explorers.

From Port Stanley, Shackleton cabled for help from Argentina and Uruguay. The Uruguayans provided a steam trawler, *Instituto de Pesca No. 1*, which picked up Shackleton at Port Stanley and got within twenty miles of the pack ice off Elephant Island. If a thick mist had lifted, the men on the island might have seen the trawler and been heartened that a rescue mission was at least in motion. But the trawler, battered by heavy seas, crept back to the Falklands unseen. A light cruiser of the Royal Navy was in port, the *Glasgow*, a veteran of the Battle of the Falkland Islands in which the German squadron under the command of vice-admiral Graf von Spee had been destroyed a few months before. The *Glasgow*'s captain was admiring of Shackleton, certainly sympathetic to his desperate desire to save his men; perhaps the *Glasgow* could be sent. A cable to the Admiralty resulted in the terse reply: "Your telegram not approved."

So Shackleton was left to fret in Port Stanley. No wonder he didn't think much of the place. He wrote in *South* that the main street "has the slaughterhouse at one end and the graveyard at the other. The chief distraction is to walk from the slaughterhouse to the graveyard. For a change one may walk from the graveyard to the slaughterhouse."

Shackleton then went to Punta Arenas in Chile, the main port on the Straits of Magellan, to try his luck there. A schooner named *Emma* with an auxiliary diesel motor was put at his disposal. With Shackleton once again on board, she was stopped 100 miles short of the pack ice. On her return, the Chileans supplied him with an ocean tug, at the time serving as a lighthouse tender, named the *Yelcho*. He must have stepped on board her with every expectation of failing once again. The *Yelcho* was only 150 tons, hardly a craft that could have dealt with the pack ice. Shackleton had to hope that he would find open seas all the way to a landfall on Elephant Island.

The situation on Elephant Island after four months was this: It was pretty much assumed that the *Caird* had been lost at sea since no rescue ship had turned up. The idea was that in October, Wild and four other members would set out in the little cutter *Dudley Docker* (dismantling the Snuggery in the process) and try to move under the lee of various islands of the South Shetlands to Deception Island in the hopes of reaching the whaling stations in the vicinity. Since most of the necessary equipment had gone to outfit the *Caird*, there was not much left for the *Dudley Docker*—a jib, old tent cloths from which to fashion a mainsail, five oars … hardly the kind of requirements needed for the estimated 250-mile journey.

On the shingled beach, the food supplies were dangerously low. Through August the main source had been limpets, little marine mollusks collected from rocks and tidal pools and shelled for food.

On August 30, the men inside the Snuggery were settling down to a meal of limpets and what was left of a boiled seal's backbone. Hurley and Marston were outside shelling when Hurley looked up: "I called Marston's attention to a curious piece of ice on the horizon, which bore a striking resemblance to

END OF RASPUTIN

December, 1916
• Members of Russia's tottering nobility assassinate Gregory Rasputin. The unordained Siberian monk from a peasant background rose to power in the royal family after Empress Alexandra became convinced he could cure her son Alexis (heir to the throne) of hemophilia.

a ship. Whilst we were so engaged a ship rounded the Gnomon Island. We immediately called out Ship O! which was instantly followed by a general exodus of cheering and semi-hysterical . . . inmates. The hoosh was left to burn and the meal forgotten."

Wild came out of the Snuggery and said of the sight, "I felt jolly well near blubbing for a bit & could not speak for several minutes." Macklin ran to the oar, which was serving as a flagpole, and tried to hoist his Burberry shirt as a signal to the boat offshore. He was able to get it up about halfway. It was what Shackleton first saw looking through his binoculars, and it immediately crossed his mind that it was a signal things had gone badly on the island. But then as the tug moved closer to land he could make out the twenty-two men onshore. Worsley remembered that moment: "He put his glasses back in their case and turned to me, his face showing more emotion than I had ever known it show before. Crean had joined us, and we were all unable to speak. It sounds trite, but years literally seemed to drop from him as he stood before us."

The *Yelcho* anchored about five hundred yards offshore, and a small boat was lowered. When it got close to the beach, the waiting men recognized Shackleton and Crean.

Shackleton never stepped ashore. "As I drew close to the rock," he wrote, "I flung packets of cigarettes ashore; they fell on them like hungry tigers, for well I knew that for months tobacco was dreamed and talked about."

Although Wild hoped he'd take a look at the Snuggery, Shackleton was worried about pack ice forming, and besides he had been superstitious about ever setting foot in what he referred to as that "Godforsaken spot."

Civilization
The rescued party in front of the Royal Hotel, Punta Arenas, Chile. Hussey, at far left, is the only one Shackleton allowed to shave before reaching port. Hurley reports that a maid at the hotel was so horrified at the sight of the grime-coated group that she left and never came back.

Orde-Lees (who else?) provides the comic relief in the midst of what must have been an emotional experience for all. With the last of the survivors aboard, Shackleton had started back for the *Yelcho*. Suddenly a man appeared at the waters' edge: Orde-Lees. He wrote of himself in the third person, "running frantically along the beach waving his arms and screaming with alarm for fear for being left behind. It would have served old 'always last' right if he had been left like Ben Gunn on Treasure Island but Sir Ernest took undeserved compassion on him and headed the boat once more for [land] and the last man to leave the accursed spot took a flying header into the boat where he arrived with a grateful…flop inflicting minor injuries on…Chilean sailors amongst whom he fell. Sir Ernest rather sarcastically congratulated him both on his punctuality and his aerial maneuvers…"

Frank Hurley had an odd reaction leaving the "noble peaks" of Elephant Island. He celebrated what he called the bliss of feeling the motion of the sea, the music of fresh though foreign voices, and to sense that their privations were ended and that they would soon be reunited with civilization. Yet he was still possessed by the experience. He writes: "I could scarcely repress feelings of sadness, to leave forever the land that has rained on us its bounty and been salvation. Our hut, a lone relic of our habitation, will become a centre around which coveys of penguins will assemble to gaze with curiosity & deliberate its origin. Good old Elephant Isle."

At Anchor

The prow of the *Yelcho* serves as a memorial in Puerto Williams, Chile to the ship and crew (with Shackleton aboard) that rescued the men of *Endurance* from Elephant Island. Exalted as they were, all had lost their sea legs and were to a man seasick on the way to Punta Arenas.

Aurora
1914—1916

I had always assumed that Shackleton's great accomplishment
—though his dream to cross the Antarctic had hardly been
realized (after all, he never set foot on the continent during
the *Endurance* expedition)—was that he had saved all his men.
This turns out not to have been quite the case, a sad fact that
emerges from the story of *Aurora*, the supply ship in McMurdo
Sound. What actually happened to the *Aurora* has been overshadowed
by the extraordinary saga of the *Endurance*.

The captain of *Aurora* and overseeing the entire operation was
a man named Aeneas Mackintosh. He had been with Shackleton
on *Nimrod* during the 1907 expedition, and in fact had lost an eye
during a cargo-loading accident. Shackleton admired him for his
resolution, his grit, his seamanship, his prior experience in the
Antarctic, and gave him command of *Aurora*. There were others—
a young Australian physicist named Dick Richards; Ernest Joyce,
experienced with dogs, had been with Scott in 1902 and Shackleton
in 1907; Ernest Wild, younger brother to Frank Wild; Vic Hayward,
the biologist, who'd had experience in the Canadian north;
and the Reverend Arnold Patrick Spencer-Smith, padre and
photographer, thirty-one years old, yet another Cambridge
graduate. Shackleton was rather suspicious of the clergy (he
referred to them as "sky pilots") but changed his mind and picked
Spencer-Smith for the *Aurora* expedition (so the rumor went)
because during his interview Spencer-Smith happened to open
his attaché case, out of which fell a woman's silk stocking and a

champagne cork. He kept entries in a small booklet Shackleton had given each member of the Ross Sea group. His first notation was a biblical quotation from Isaiah: "Thus saith the Lord, Heaven is my throne, the earth my footstool. Where is the House that ye built unto me? And where is my place of rest?"

Then, almost as if spoofing the solemnity of what he'd written, he added, "It's all in the game. Play on!"

Very British!

Aurora left Hobart, Tasmania, for the South on Christmas Day. *Endurance* had sailed from South Georgia three weeks earlier. As soon as landfall was established on Ross Island, three camps were prepared. The largest and most commodious was Cape Evans, that Scott had built in 1910—windowed, insulated floors, bunks in tiers of two, lighting through an acetylene generator, an area for a laboratory, and a partitioned cubicle that Scott had set aside for himself. The second was at Hut Point, thirteen miles across the sea ice, a far more primitive structure, and then finally Safety Camp, a desolate staging area from where the final parties would set out for the south.

Mackintosh decided that depots had to be laid down as soon as possible in case Shackleton and his party had made a landing and were already on their way. Shackleton's orders had been to lay a depot of supplies at the 80th parallel. Mackintosh set off from Safety Camp with a small party, six in all to begin with, and then moving on with Wild and Joyce with utmost difficulty he managed to reach the 80th parallel, not far from where Scott, Bowers, Wilson, and Oates had lost their lives in 1912. At each parallel along the way they left depots made of cut blocks of ice, packed to heights of about twelve feet, a twenty-foot pole stuck in the top with a black flag attached to stand out from afar against the snow. Also, along the way smaller cairns were constructed to mark the route, welcome sights to spot on the return trip.

But they had a wretched time. By the time they returned to Hut Point they had lost all nine of the dogs they'd taken with them. Ernest Wild lost the top of one ear, and part of a big toe had to be amputated.

Worse still, when they reached the main camp at Cape Evans, where the rest of the expedition had been waiting, they heard the news that *Aurora* had suddenly disappeared during a gale. Richards explained what had happened—that at 3 A.M. on the early morning of May 7 he had stepped outside to take a weather reading. A faint moon was shining. From the door of the hut a familiar sight had been the top masts of *Aurora* where she was moored to the shore. There were no masts to be seen. He hurried down to the beach. Her snapped hawsers were lying twisted and broken on the shore. A blizzard sweeping out of the south had pushed the ice pack with *Aurora* in it away from the

In Charge

Aurora's one-eyed captain, Aenas Mackintosh (left), and Ernest Wild, whose brother Frank was serving on *Endurance* on the other side of the continent at the same time.

shore, a vast tonnage of ice moving her hopelessly entrapped up the McMurdo Sound toward the Ross Sea.

He rushed back to Camp Evans and announced to the startled men within, "She's gone. The ship's gone. The wind has taken her out."

Aboard the ship nothing could be done, a parallel situation to what was going on with *Endurance* in the Weddell Sea. Chief Officer John Stenhouse wrote in his log, "We are drifting God knows where! But what of the poor beggars at Cape Evans—and the returning Southern party? It is a dismal prospect for them."

✧　　✧　　✧

JOURNAL ENTRY, 2002 • *Paradise Cove, Antarctic Peninsula*

As I was getting ready to step into the Zodiac, a half mile away a side of the glacier fell away with a roar that reached our ears a second or so later and turned heads everywhere to the shore. There we glimpsed the great slab drop into the sea, sending up a great plume of snow to temporarily hide the scar on the glacier where it had been. I don't think anyone who saw that sight did not instantly equate what they had just seen with the collapse of the twin towers of the World Trade Center a few months before—no cries of wonderment at one of nature's great sights, but a kind of gloom settling over the ship. No talk as we stand away from the side of the ship.

Unlucky *Aurora*

An Antarctic veteran, she leaked badly. After she left Newcastle, Australia, in June 1917 she disappeared without a trace in the Southern Ocean.

OSCAR

• The dogs on the *Aurora* expedition were led by a massive-headed husky named Oscar, after Oscar Wilde, or more likely a play on words after Ernest Wild. Oscar was R.W. Richards's favorite—"an old reprobate, a dirty dog if you like, a quick-tempered brute, but he was always there when the chips were down, pulling his heart in front of the others." Oscar spent his declining years in a New Zealand zoo, and didn't die until 1939—his long life a tribute to his canine brethren who had perished in the name of exploration.

✧　✧　✧

The *Aurora* was held fast in the ice for ten months. The same kind of vise-crushing activity of the ice floes that caused *Endurance* to founder also beset *Aurora*, destroying the rudder, damaging the propeller. Finally, in March 1916, she was able to push into open water and set sail for New Zealand, one thousand miles to the north. Weakened by the buffeting of storms and the crush of ice during her entrapment, she eventually eased into Port Chalmers.

Back at Cape Evans, one of the expedition, Irvine Gaze, summed it up. "We won't see her back this year—if ever. We have to face it. We are marooned."

The situation didn't keep the Ross Ice party from carrying out their orders. Mackintosh and his men spent the winter getting ready to move south and set up more depots. Much of the time was spent sledging supplies from Cape Evans to Hut Point and beyond to Safety Camp. The final party consisted of Spencer-Smith, Richards, Joyce, Hayward, Mackintosh, and Ernest Wild. They passed the 83rd parallel, where Shackleton eight years before had turned back from his Furthest South. Spencer-Smith became too weak to go on, hardly able to move because of the effects of scurvy. He was finally left in a small tent to be retrieved on the return trip. He kept notes in his diary for the week he was left alone. He described a hallucinatory dream in which he was told the war was over and the German rivers were now English, in another that "we met Sir Ernest and Frank Wild with one motor and one dog sledge, both clean and neat, and F.W. wearing a very much gold-laced cap, Sir F. clean-shaven." He wrote that he had concocted a comedy in his head but it was so cold he could not write it down. One entry read, "Spent day delivering a lecture and a sermon—in execrable French."

The others moved on thirty miles and reached Mt. Hope at the foot of the Beardmore Glacier. Mackintosh, rambling and confused, had faded from command. Joyce had become the nominal leader. He wrote, "I picked a place which would not be missed by any one coming from the south." A depot of two weeks' food and fuel

No Dogs Please, We're British
Members of the Ross Ice Shelf party in the traces, pulling a sledge of depot supplies across the barren plain. Men (as opposed to dogs) hauling supplies across the ice was the classic British style of exploration.

THE WIND

A view from the space shuttle *Columbia* of katabatic flow clouds.

The strongest winds on earth exist on Antarctica. Known as katabatics, they are caused by the colder air of the plateau sliding down to the coast at terrific speeds, up to 150 mph. Cherry-Garrard wrote of such winds, "I have never heard or felt or seen a wind like this. I wonder why it did not carry away the earth." An interesting reading was made during one of the Byrd expeditions when a pilot got into a moored airplane to make a radio call and noted that the airspeed indicator inside the cockpit read 140 kilometers per hour.

An Antarctic blizzard, on the other hand, is not what we think of in everyday terms; often no snow falls; strong winds pick the snow off the surface and blow the fine, needle-like particles in blinding sheets, often causing a condition known as white-out, where one can't see more than a foot or so (lives have been lost within easy walking distance of shelter) and loses any sense of where the horizon is. A friend of mine described it as very much like losing one's bearings scuba-diving at night in ink-black seas and being unable to tell whether one is going up or down.

was left for Shackleton's party. Ernest Wild wrote a letter to his brother, Frank, and left it for him to find.

Spencer-Smith was still alive in his tent when they came back for him. He wrote, "Laus Deo [Praise the Lord]! It is strange but cheery to hear men and dogs again." He was too weak to walk, so was tucked into a sleeping bag and strapped to one of the sledges. Joyce often looked back in forlorn hope that Shackleton had made it across the Pole and was catching up with them. "...I very often looked wistfully to the south to see if by any chance Shackleton was coming up."

One hundred miles from Hut Point, Mackintosh and Hayward joined Spencer-Smith as invalids. To lessen the load for the stronger men and dogs to haul, Mackintosh was left behind in a tent to be retrieved later.

They proceeded north. Dick Richards gives a memorable sense of what it was like: "Trudging along, hour after hour, day after day, with a canvas harness over the shoulders and round the waist is a fantastic experience ... There was no conversation on the trail. Each step forward was a little advance on the last ... All our energies were needed for the job in hand. The silence was profound; the soft crunch of feet in the snow, the faint swish of the sledge runners serving only to emphasize that silence ... The hours of a day's march seemed endless. I do not know what went on in the minds of my companions while on the march over these months ... in my case I'd perform long useless computations of one sort or another in my head ... an automatic reaction of the monotony that was forced upon us, an anodyne to the weariness of the body. We seldom thought about the outside world. We had heard nothing of it since December 1914. We had left all that behind. The outside seemed unreal; the only reality we had was what we saw about us."

Joyce writes an equally vivid account: "If I were in civilization I would not venture two yards...the blisters on my foot were as large as potatoes...I ask myself why on earth one comes to this part of the earth. Here we are, frostbitten in the day, frozen at night. What a life!"

Spencer-Smith did not survive. Richards' account of his death is brief: "At 6 A.M. on the morning of March 9 when we rose [the five men were crowded into a three-man tent] he had been dead for some little time, as ice had formed on his eyelashes and beard."

Richards and Wild took turns digging a trench in the snow. The tent was taken down. Among them there wasn't enough strength to pick up the padre's body and settle it into his grave. They could only roll the dead body over and over until it reached the grave and fell in. A crude cross was erected from bamboo sticks. Wild promised that he would return to the Barrier and put up a more suitable memorial.

In mid-March they finally reached the secondary camp at Hut Point to wait until the conditions made it possible to cross the bay to Camp Evans. Life there is hard to imagine. Richards in his memoir writes: "The sole food we had from the middle of March until the middle of July—four whole months—was seal meat. That is all we had—morning, noon, and night...we would throw those blocks...into the fire and they would melt and flare and some of the fat would run down through the cracks between the bricks and across the floor. When this was thick enough, we would scrape it into a tin of some kind and use it for lighting. A piece of string or a strip of cloth would float in the melting fat and burn and give us a crude kind of candle. It was then coming on to 24 hours of darkness every day and these burning wicks were all we had to see by. On the days when the wind veered and the blubber smoke filled the spot we could see almost nothing.

Richards described this as "living the life of primitive troglodytes."

Mackintosh and Hayward suddenly decided it was too much for them. A constant diet of fresh meat had almost cured them of scurvy. They thought themselves capable of travel. On the morning of May 8 they decided to cross the pack ice thirteen miles to Cape Evans. Company was there, food, warmth, a palace compared to where they were. Neither Richards or Joyce thought it a good idea. The ice in the bay tended to break up in heavy weather, pushed away from the shore by the wind coming

Keep off the Ice
Contemporary Antarctic travelers look out on the stretch of sea ice from Cape Evans—the area in which Mackintosh and Heyward disappeared. Even in the severest cold weather, the depth and strength of such a surface is hardly predictable, and is constantly changed by the relentless wind and currents.

out of the south, and float up McMurdo Sound. Joyce was convinced a blizzard was on the way and said as much to Macintosh: "You may call me 'old cautious' but I would not go to Cape Evans today for all the tea in China."

Hayward looked dubious, but Macintosh was adamant and finally Hayward gave in and went with him.

"I can see these two figures now quite clearly in my mind's eye," Richards wrote afterward, "They appeared pigmy-like as they grew fainter in the dim light against the vast expanse of sea ice to the north, and we watched them for a while in silence."

Sure enough, the blizzard Joyce had predicted moved into the area and confined the pair to the hut for four days. "When the weather moderated, in the dim light, we traced their steps raised up in the salty ice for about three miles to the north, where they ended abruptly in the young ice just forming."

They attempted the crossing themselves eight weeks later. It was a cloudless night, very cold, with a full moon to light their way. The ice held, but then something happened that must have terrified them until they realized what was going on: objects bright in the moonlight slowly began to fade into darkness, the landscape vanishing into a sepulchral gloom. At first they must have thought their eyes were giving them trouble... until they realized that by the utmost chance their crossing coincided with a total eclipse of the moon! Joyce looked up and exclaimed, "By God—look at that!"

A further surprise came when their approach to Cape Evans was greeted by a much larger group of dogs than they had expected. "We had completely forgotten that we had left the bitch with a prospective litter, that these pups who had been born at the base were quite big dogs now.

Petermann Island

On the southeast coast of Petermann Island, the *Explorer* holds in a cove defined by Point Circumcision. The spot was discovered on New Year's Day, 1909 by Jean-Baptiste Charcot, who gave it that somewhat exacting name after the holy day of the Feast of the Circumcision, when tradition tells us Christ was circumcised. Charcot spent the winter there on his ship, *Pourquoi Pas?*, which had electric lighting and a 1,500-volume library. The *Pourquoi Pas?* was his second ship. While he was away on the first (the *Français*) his wife divorced him. He took his second wife with him on *Pourquoi Pas?* as far as Punta Arenas, having already persuaded her to sign a prenuptial agreement that she would not oppose his explorations.

I could see them with their fur silhouetted in faint prismatic colours in the light of the returning moon."

The first question they asked was about Macintosh and Hayward. Their worst fears were confirmed. The two hadn't made it, no sign of them. It had to be assumed that the two men had either slipped into the weakening ice, or had been carried off on a floe, ever diminishing, up McMurdo Sound toward the Ross Sea.

✧ ✧ ✧

Safe Haven
The refuge hut, its foundations pretty much occupied by gentoo penguins, was built by the Argentinians in 1955 on a spot close to where Charcot spent the winter of 1909.

JOURNAL ENTRY, 2002 • *Lemaire Channel, Petermann Island*
We sail slowly down the Lemaire Channel, a narrow passage between a series of mountainous islands and the Antarctic Peninsula. We went ashore on Petermann Island. There's a small rescue hut on there, built by the Argentinians on the site where Jean-Baptiste Charcot wintered in 1909 (the Second French Antarctic Expedition) from his wonderfully named ship, *Pourquoi Pas? (Why Not?)* —a winter here with his wines and his comparatively grand living style. We were told a register was inside. A group from the *Explorer* walked through the snow to look it over. Bob and I decided to take our own tour, a tough walk for me through the crust that breaks underfoot, up to the knee. Very easy to leave a yellow boot behind as a permanent relic.

At the rescue hut gentoo penguins are everywhere, almost as if ready to take over occupancy as soon as someone comes along and opens the door for them. We had been told to stay out of the place unless with the group but Bob, of course, went in to look around and perhaps sign the register. He came out and told me what was in there—a guitar on the wall, missing a string or two; mementoes and plaques from the various ships that had visited, a Pole and a Russian among them; several bunk beds in the back; cans of food, coffee, and condiments like salt, pepper, and honey; a wood stove and some wood…a kind of recently lived-in feeling and the smell of a campfire.

Afterward, we heard that three English mountaineers had taken refuge there a few years before after an unsuccessful attempt to climb Mount Scott, which rears up abruptly across the channel. Driven back by avalanches, they had crossed solid ice to the rescue hut, but then, attempting to get

back to the Mount Scott side to try to reach a communications station fifty miles south, the ice had broken up on the way and they had drifted down the channel—three men on an ice floe, no way of propelling it to land, a most dismal situation to consider. Apparently they wrote what they intended to do in the register, and since they disappeared without a trace, it must be assumed that floating out to sea, three figures so insignificant in that vastness of ice, was indeed their fate. The *Lonely Planet* guide has a warning about such a condition—that the best thing to do is swim hard for the bottom since drowning is preferable to freezing to death.

Memorial
On Windvane Hill above Scott's *Terra Nova* hut at Cape Evans is a memorial to the three members of the Ross Ice Shelf party who perished during Shackleton's Trans-Continental Expedition. The figure in the hooded raiment is Britain's Princess Anne, on a February 2002 visit to commemorate the centenary of Scott's arrival in the Antarctic.

✧ ✧ ✧

For those at Cape Evans, it was now a question of waiting for rescue. Such was the admiration for Shackleton that one wrote, "We didn't know whether the Boss would come overland from the south or by sea from the north. We only knew that he would come."

Shackleton reached Port Chalmers in New Zealand in early December to make arrangements to rescue the Ross Ice Shelf party. He found that the *Aurora* had been repaired and refitted during the year; just over a month after he arrived, he was aboard *Aurora* moving up McMurdo Sound.

It was Richards who spotted the rescue ship. He was on a rise near the flank of Mount Erebus when he spotted some movement in the ice to the north, nothing that startled him particularly because icebergs often shifted in the currents; perhaps it was a seal on a floe. He put his binoculars to his eyes to take a look. "It seemed that at the very time I started to look through the glasses, a stoker threw some fresh coal on the furnace, and there was a belch of black smoke curling into the air. Then I knew there was a ship."

The men at Cape Evans, sitting along the length of a mess table, at first thought it was a bad joke when Richards walked in and nonchalantly announced, "There's a ship out there."

Wild excitement, of course. The men raced down toward the shore to meet their rescuers. There were two wondrous moments—the realization that that the ship standing offshore was their old friend *Aurora*, not at the

bottom of the Ross Sea as they feared, and that one of three men who had come ashore and approaching was Shackleton himself, coming not out of the south, as planned so long ago, but the north.

A strange aspect of the meeting was that after a quick exchange of greetings, Shackleton and the two men with him moved off to one side and lay flat on the ice—a pre-arranged signal to those aboard *Aurora* to indicate how many of the original party had died. Odd if there had been more than three. One of the men, or more if the casualties had been higher, presumably would have stood up and then laid down again in the snow for a second time.

The captain of *Aurora*, John King Davis, gives a vivid description of the Ross Ice Shelf party coming aboard. "We expected that they would be unkempt. I had not fully appreciated what a profound effect such a long period of isolation could have on their appearance. They were just about the wildest-looking gang of men I had ever seen in my life. Smoke-bleared eyes looked out from grey haggard faces; their hair was matted and uncut, their beards impregnated with soot and grease... Their great physical suffering went deeper than their appearance. Their speech was jerky, at times semi-hysterical, almost unintelligible. Their eyes had a strained harassed look—and no wonder! These events had rendered these hapless individuals as unlike ordinary human beings as any I have ever met. The Antarctic had given them the full treatment."

Apparently when the rescued contingent sat down to eat in the confined quarters of *Aurora*'s wardroom, the smell was so bad that some of their hosts had to step outside. They heard Shackleton talk about Endurance, the voyage of the James Caird, the rescue by the Chileans without a man of the expedition lost, and, of course, the news that while their own struggles were going on, that the rest of the world was embroiled in the terrible slaughter of the Great War.

The first land attempt to duplicate what Shackleton hoped to do in 1915 was made in 1958 by the scholar-explorer Sir Vivian Fuchs and Edmund Hillary, who had been the first to reach the peak of Mount Everest. Fuchs's plan was to follow the Shackleton route, more or less, starting from the Weddell Sea, and Hillary, on the other side of the continent, was to supply the depots Fuchs would need once he'd reached the South Pole and started north to the Ross Ice Shelf—very much the task Shackleton had assigned the men aboard *Aurora*. Coinciding

WILSON AGAIN

• Campaigning under the slogan "He Kept Us Out of War," U.S. President Woodrow Wilson is re-elected in 1916. The race against former Supreme Court Justice Charles Evans Hughes is so close that many papers call Hughes the winner. However, Wilson asks Congress to declare war on Germany in April 1917.

Fellow Adventurers
Sir Edmund Hillary (left) and Sir Vivian Fuchs in 1957. Fuchs was the first man to complete what Shackleton set out to do—cross over the South Pole on a route from the Weddell Sea to McMurdo Sound.

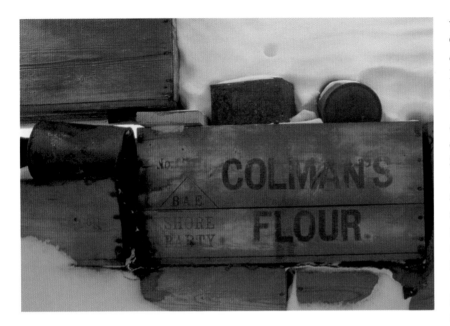

Detritus
Old wooden crates stand in the snow outside Scott's Hut at Cape Evans. The restoration has kept everything much as it was when the *Aurora* party was there in 1915-17.

with the International Geophysical Year, it was described as "the last great land journey to be undertaken on earth."

It is interesting to compare the two expeditions. In *Endurance* Shackleton had arrived in the Antarctic with sixty or so dogs and one cat, but since he never set foot on the mainland, none were of any practical use save as food for his men.

The *Aurora* group, having lost most of their dogs on an ill-advised reconnaissance, only had four dogs to help haul their sledges to set up the depots.

Sir Edmund Hillary, on the other hand, arrived at approximately the same starting-off point with sixty dogs, seven tractors, including three Sno-Cats, and a Beaver recconaissance aircraft. The U.S. Navy lent them an icebreaker to clear the route through the pack ice to the shore, along with a helicopter to help with the recconaissance. What's more, all hands knew that the Americans had a polar station at the South Pole, with a laboratory, mess hall, dormitories, and warmth and fresh food awaiting.

Speaking of food, compare 1958 and the *Aurora* Ross Ice Shelf party in 1917.

THE FUCHS-HILLARY EXPEDITION:
Breakfast: Cereals and apricots; bacon and scrambled eggs
Lunch: Tomatoes purée, cold roast lamb, mashed potatoes, fruit salad
Dinner: Game soup, curry entrée, roast beef and Yorkshire pudding, roast parsnip, boiled onions, mashed potatoes, tinned green beans, boiled pudding and custard

THE ROSS ICE SHELF PARTY NEARING THE HUT:
Breakfast: one cup of tea, half biscuit
Lunch: tea, half biscuit
Dinner: quarter biscuit, tea, scraping of food bag

The Fuchs team from the Weddell Sea had a particularly difficult time, slowed in part by the considerable size of his convoy—four Sno-Cats, three Weasels, a Muskeg (all tracked vehicles to deal with the snow), along with dog teams to reconnoiter the trail ahead. His route was crisscrossed with crevasses and potholes—many of them covered with a bank of snow that could support a man on skis or a dog team, perhaps, but not a vehicle. The giveaway to a crevasse were tadpole-shaped depressions in the snow. Six-foot long aluminum

poles were then brought out and poked in the snow. If they still met resistance six feet down, the crevasse bridge was assumed to be sturdy enough to support the vehicles, some of which, the Sno-Cats, weighed over three tons. Sometimes the vibration of their engines as the vehicles came up to one of these "tadpoles" would cause the bridge over a crevasse to collapse, a gap half the size of a tennis court suddenly and soundlessly opening up ahead. The solution was to link the tractors with three-inch cables so that if one slid into a crevasse it could be hauled out by the others. Because of such problems, on one occasion the day's run was limited to a scant half-mile.

Hillary and his people had a much easier time of it. In fact, when he reached the American station at the Pole he learned that Fuchs was still three hundred miles away; he worried that Fuchs would arrive too late to continue down to the Ross Ice Shelf and that he might have to spend the winter at the American base before continuing on. He suggested as much to Fuchs over the radio. Fortunately, on January 6 Fuchs' party came to an area free of crevasses and the wind-sharpened ridges called sastrugi; they were able to average thirty miles a day. Hillary, waiting for them at the Pole, describes the meeting:

"What an imposing sight they were! Every vehicle and sledge had a flag flying as they swept up at high speed to come to a halt beside us. Bunny [Fuchs] jumped out of the leading Sno-Cat and we shook hands and exchanged greetings. We drove back to the Pole Station in some disorder but in high spirits."

Then after four days rest at the Polar Station, Fuchs, with Hillary leading, left for the Ross Ice Shelf and McMurdo Sound. Averaging thirty miles a day, they reached

Set to Go
Equipment, including a pile of sledges, for the British Commonwealth Trans-Antarctic Expedition in 1957 waits at McMurdo Sound. Sir Edmund Hillary's team of New Zealanders were outfitted with modified farm tractors that he had suggested as being suitable for polar travel.

their objective in a little over a month, the Sno-Cats pulling up to the encampment at Scott's Base on March 2 —thus completing what Shackleton had hoped to do forty-three years before.

The reception accorded the expedition's arrival at McMurdo is hardly comparable to that of the early explorers staggering in to accept with trembling hands a cup of hoosh.

Here are Fuchs and Hillary describing their arrival: "As we ran in toward the island, we began to pick out the huts of Scott Base against the dark rock of Pram Point; then Weasels, Ferguson tractors and Bren gun carriers [tracked vehicles adopted from a military model] could be seen streaming out along the track to meet us. Soon we joined up, and as the Sno-Cats thundered and weaved between the ridges, escorted in front by and behind a variety of vehicles, scores of figures stood, camera in hand, at every vantage point."

Congratulations

Hillary and Fuchs (above) shake hands as the latter arrives at the South Pole from the Weddell Sea. In the background and on the opposite page is a Tucker Sno-Cat vehicle.

Equivalently, the men aboard *Aurora* would have crowded the shore to meet Shackleton coming down the Ross Ice Shelf with all his people! So the question comes up. Suppose Shackleton had made a successful landing at Vahsel Bay and immediately set off across the continent as he planned? Fuchs wrote of this decision, "I do not believe that was ever a practical idea because unsupported travelling with dog teams would have required at least three months, averaging 20 miles a day to cover his estimated 1,800 miles to the Ross Sea . . . a thousand miles before reaching a depot—even if the Ross Sea party had been able to place one at the head of the Beardmore Glacier."

What if Shackleton had reconsidered and spend that first austral summer of 1915 with the *Endurance* moored and reconnoitered southward, establishing one or two depots inland, and then, after spending the winter aboard his ship, setting off in the spring of 1916?

Even then, Fuchs was doubtful. He wrote, "I have been compelled to assume travelling conditions would have been good, that the dog teams would have been efficiently trained and properly fed; and above all, that the drivers would have been experienced. If one takes into account the terrible storys of the support party's experience, I fear these assumptions are open to considerable doubt . . . the weather even at the height of summer was atrocious on the Ross Ice Shelf.

"If these factors had affected Shackleton's party his chances of success would have been small, indeed. It may therefore be permissible"—and what a telling sentence this is!—"that the loss of the *Endurance* may have saved a worse disaster."

Quest
1917–1922

Although news of Shackleton's survival caused a brief sensation in Europe, his welcome home in May 1917 was understandably muted, given the war—quite a comedown after his heroic return from the *Nimrod* expedition. He hoped to get some sort of commission in the war effort but he was legally exempt at age 43, one year over the conscription limit. Almost everyone else in the expedition quickly found themselves in the war.

Many signed on to minesweepers; some from the *Aurora* fought with the New Zealand forces. Macklin served as a medical officer in Italy. Frank Wild also fought in Europe. Hussey was an artilleryman in France. In the Royal Navy, Worsley won the Distinguished Service Order after his ship destroyed a German submarine.

The most tragic case was McCarthy, who, after surviving the open-boat crossing of the *James Caird*, died in the English Channel while manning a gun. Two members of the *Aurora* crew also died in combat: a carpenter named Mauger and Frank Wild's brother Ernest, killed on a minesweeper in the Mediterranean. Five more expedition members were wounded, including McIlroy, who was badly hurt at Ypres.

Unable to find himself any kind of active military service— he refused to take a physical, which might have exposed his bad heart—Shackleton approached his connections in the government and secured a diplomatic position in Buenos Aires. His job was to try to persuade the governments of Argentina and Chile to give

up their status of neutrality and enter the war on the Allied side. In Argentina, he thought the best way to do this was to influence the president—a task that was not easy. He wrote to Lord Robert Cecil, undersecretary of state for foreign affairs, that the president "lives in four rooms over a bootblack shop, having refused on his election to reside in Government House. In his house live his Austrian mistress and his illegitimate daughter. Neither has any influence over him."

Shackleton's South American posting was almost surely an attempt by the British government to keep him at a distance. He was gaining a reputation as a heavy drinker, something of a maverick, and career foreign service types were openly critical of his freewheeling methods as an amateur diplomat. Nothing came of his attempts to engage the president, or anyone else of substance, in Argentina, and he returned home in March 1918.

By then the Bolsheviks had taken over Russia and negotiated a separate peace with Germany, which included handing over the strategic Arctic Sea island of Spitsbergen. The British government decided on an undercover operation to secure a presence in Spitsbergen (since its status was somewhat unclear), and Shackleton (along with McIlroy, recovered from his battle wounds) was sent there under the guise of mineral exploration. In northern Norway on the way to Spitsbergen, Shackleton suffered a probable heart attack and was forced to return home.

His last attempt in service for his country was to handle supply and maintenance at Murmansk, the only ice-free Russian port in the north, then under British control. With the war still going on, the Allies feared a polar winter at Murmansk was inevitable; Shackleton was a good choice, as someone who understood survival in extreme conditions. The war ended two weeks after his arrival, but he decided to stay, once again trying to set up business in a mining venture. The Bolsheviks had not yet taken control of the country's polar regions, and many observers—including Shackleton—hoped northern Russia could be "saved" as a country unto itself. After the brutality of the Bolsheviks became evident in the murder of the tsar and his family, Shackleton and almost all other foreigners left in March 1919.

Back in London, Shackleton began drinking and smoking even more heavily. He gained weight. He gave some lectures to make ends meet, but the halls were often only half-filled. His subject was the romance of polar expeditions. He rarely spent time at home.

Spellbinder

In April 1917, Shackleton (posing in New York) gave a lecture at Carnegie Hall about his country. The talk moved one listener, an Anglo-Irishman named Sir Shane Leslie, to recall in an interview with Shackleton biographer James Fisher that it was "the most exciting, tremendous meeting I ever attended in the United States…I've never felt the audience played on like an organ by a man talking except Winston [Churchill] and Shackleton, and… it hardly mattered what they said."

In 1919 his memoir *South* was published. He had dictated the contents to Edward Saunders, a New Zealander, who had helped him write an earlier work about the *Nimrod* expedition entitled *The Heart of the Antarctic*. He didn't enjoy writing. He once told his wife, "I can talk much better than I can write." He would pace up and down for an hour or so, barking out sentences in short staccato bursts, that Saunders, a trained reporter, would transcribe and improve. (That had also been the procedure with *The Heart of the Antarctic*.) Leonard Hussey helped with the final editing.

The critics praised *South*, especially Apsley Cherry-Garrard in *The Nation*, but the proceeds went to pay off those who had put up the money for *Endurance*.

In the frigid stretches north of Murmansk he had written Stancomb-Wills a poignant letter in which he describes his feelings being once again in the polar regions. "The very first . . . snow-squalls bring home to us the memories of our old South Lands. There is freshness in the air, a briskness in the breeze that renews one's youth."

Perhaps it was inevitable that once again he would turn south.

In early 1921 Shackleton acquired a converted Norwegian sealer named *Foca 1*. It was a somewhat humdrum name, and at the suggestion of Emily, it was changed to *Quest*. The financing came from an old school friend at Dulwich, John Quiller Rowett, whose fortune came from rum; indeed he was rumored to have cornered most of the world's supply.

The reasons for the voyage are obscure. Shackleton was restless, for sure, bothered by financial woes, unhappy with marital life, bored. There were purported reasons: He proposed to Rowett that he was going to circumnavigate the Antarctic looking for "lost" islands. Always he'd had ideas about finding treasure, Captain Kidd's, said to be somewhere on South Trinidad in the

EXPRESSIONIST CINEMA

November 14, 1921
• Robert Wiene's *The Cabinet of Dr. Caligari* opens in Paris on November 14, 1921. The German expressionist film, about a mad psychiatrist who hypnotizes people into committing murder, uses deep shadows and stylized acting to reflect on abuses of power.

SKI MARATHON

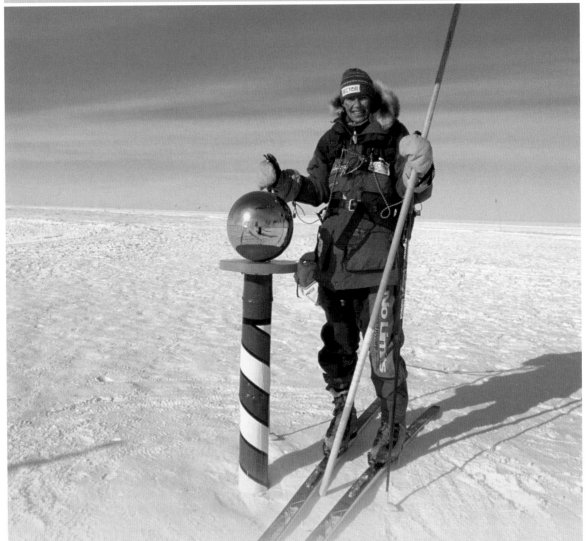

On Christmas morning, 1994, Norwegian Liv Arnesen holds her country's flag at a marker at the South Pole—the first woman to ski alone to the Pole. She returned by aircraft.

In the Antarctic summer of 1989–90, two men, an Austro-Italian mountain climber named Reinhold Messner and a German, Arved Fuchs (no relation to Sir Vivian Fuchs) skiied across Antarctica from the Weddell Sea to Ross Island, more or less taking the same route Shackleton had planned. An aircraft had left them supply depots along the way to the Pole. But from the Pole to the Ross Sea (along the path of Scott's doomed expedition), the plan was to forgo any depots. They pared down the weight on their lightweight plastic sledges, leaving out even radios. Using para-sails when the wind was right, they traveled almost one hundred miles a day. (One matches this against their slowpoke predecessors: the best Amundsen could do was fourteen). They completed the trip in ninety-two days.

In 1992, a Norwegian cross-country skier named Erling Kagge skied solo to the Pole without any supply depots along the route. He reached the Pole without incident. I doubt the thought occurred to him to continue on. He was picked up by a plane at the Pole and flown back to home base.

Atlantic…or to find a pearl lagoon in the Pacific. He had a notion gold was to be found somewhere in the Antarctic; he had brought back mud from the Ross Sea rescue trip and had it appraised for gold, of which there was none. He was fond of the aphorism about the two stages in the life of the diver: *"One when a beggar he prepares to plunge, / One when a prince he rises with his pearl."*

Most likely he could not help himself. He writes, "Besides there's a peculiar fascination about going— I don't think I can explain it in words—but there's an excitement, a thrill—a sort of magnetic attraction about polar exploration."

Antarctic Skiff
This collapsible boat was carried aboard the *Quest*. As with the expedition itself, the portable craft's actual purpose was unclear.

The urge would seem to be revealed in three of his favorite poems. Indeed, read in order they encapsulate his entire life—the lure of exploration, the inevitability of failure. The first is by Robert W. Service (which surely must have inspired Robert Frost to write his famous "The Road Not Taken"):

The trails of the world be countless, and most of the trails be tried,
You tread on the heels of many, till you come to where the ways divide,
And one he's safe as the sunlight, and the other is dreary and wan,
Yet you look askant on the Lone Trail, yet the Lone Trail lures you on . . .

And this from St. John Lucas:
We were the fools who could not rest
In the dull earth we left behind
But burned with passion for the South
And drank strange frenzy from the wind.
The world where wise men sit at ease
Fades from my unregretful eyes
And blind across uncharted seas
We stagger on our enterprise

And finally, another Robert W. Service:
I have flouted the Wild, I have followed its lure
Fearless, familiar, alone.
But a day must come when the Wild will win
And I shall be overthrown.

He called for his "Old Guard" to join him—eight of them, even Green, the cook on *Endurance*, turned up: Leonard Hussey, the banjo player and jokesmith, perhaps Shackleton's closest friend; Kerr, the second engineer;

Macklin, the chief surgeon who had helped operate on Percy Blackborrow's gangrenous toes; McLeod, the Scottish seaman who refused to eat penguins because he thought they contained the souls of dead fishermen; McIlroy, the second surgeon who actually performed the Blackborrow operation; Frank Wild of Elephant Island, and Frank Worsley, *Endurance's* captain, the master of navigational skills who was, of course, on the *James Caird*. Others who might have gone were tempted but for various reasons—often simply a matter of not being able to spend the time, or being too far away—sent their regrets. McNeish ignored the matter completely. It is said he never forgave Shackleton for ordering the execution of Mrs. Chippy. Also, he must have known that Shackleton had never recommended him for the highly valued Polar Medal, probably because of the unpleasantness at Patience Camp.

From the diaries kept by some of those aboard *Quest* it is evident that Shackleton was not himself, indeed in alarming ill-health. He began drinking in the morning, very likely to deaden the pains of angina attacks. In Rio de Janeiro he was hit with an obvious heart attack but would not let himself be examined, once again avoiding the stethoscope as if it was a snake. In his own diary he wrote a forlorn passage: "Ah me: The years that have gone since in the pride of young manhood I first went forth to the fight. I grow old and tired but must always lead on."

On the 4th of January *Quest* reached South Georgia. As she sailed along the coast, Shackleton and Worsley showed those from *Endurance*—who had never seen where the final act of the drama had been played out—the various points of interest ... where they had traversed the mountains from King Haakon Bay to Stromness.

The ship anchored in Cumberland Bay, just off the whaling station at Grytviken. That night Shackleton went ashore for a reunion with those who eight years before had welcomed him back to civilization. Back on board ship he wrote in his journal that he'd had "a wonderful evening."

The last entry reads: "In the darkening twilight I saw a lone star hover gem-like above the bay."

That night in his cabin he had trouble sleeping and called for Hussey. "Huss ... play me some of the old tunes will you. They always help me sleep."

Macklin came to see him and, worried about the heart attack in Rio de Janeiro, suggested that he ought to change his way of life. "You 're always wanting me to give up things," Shackleton commented. "What is it I ought to give up."

Those were his last words. In the early morning, Shackleton suffered another heart attack and died. He was forty-seven.

His body was sent to Montevideo aboard the whale factory ship with the odd name *Professor Gravel*, destined for England, but was then returned to South Georgia at the request of Emily. The internment at the little cemetery at Grytviken took place on March 5, 1922. He lies with the whaling men.

He had written Emily on one occasion: "Sometimes I think I am no good at anything but being away in the wilds just with men."

At the news of Shackleton's death, Orde-Lees wrote from Japan: "I should like to know a little about his best wishes and the resting place of his noble soul."

✧ ✧ ✧

JOURNAL ENTRY, 2002 • *Aboard the* Explorer

Before the *Explorer* sailed for the Drake Passage, we picked up certificates at the purser's office with our names in curlicue script attesting that we had set foot on the Antarctic continent. Suitable for framing. I went up to the bar and had a gin rickey. I can't remember the last time I had such a thing. It sounds like the kind of drink one orders on safari, at some outpost far from home. Yet looking out on the sunlit bay, there was no way I could equate my stay in these parts with anything I'd read about Shackleton or any of the other explorers. It might have helped if we'd gone through a blizzard, or a kanataki had roared down out of the hills. The *Explorer*'s captain could not remember a series of days as perfect. He had thought it a wonder we had been able to land on Elephant Island, where often cruise ships wallow in heavy seas for hours before giving up. My most serious problem (other than the confrontation with the fur seal) had been how to get in and out of my Wellington boots.

ANNIE GETS HER GUN

March 5, 1922
• 61-year-old sharpshooter Annie Oakley breaks the record for women's trap shooting—by breaking 98 out of 100 clay targets at 16 yards. Oakley began shooting at age 9, and later joined Buffalo Bill's Wild West Show, where she became an international star.

Funeral Cortege

When news came to Montevideo that Shackleton's body was to be returned to South Georgia, an impressive ceremonial procession was organized by the Uruguayans. His coffin rests on a gun carriage draped with the Uruguayan flag.

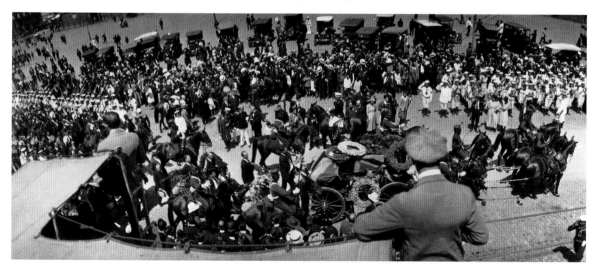

Of course, there had been disappointments. I had seen the South Georgia pipit but not the emperor penguin. Nor the carnivorous duck. I had pretty much consigned the latter to being a hoax after one of the tour guides told me about a large hot-blooded rat that lived in the ice, like a mole. Trying to keep his face straight, the guide said that to feed, the rat placed itself under a penguin and melted the ice with its body warmth. The penguin tumbles down and is consumed.

"Oh yes," I said.

He admitted reading about this rat in a scientific journal, an April Fool's joke as it turned out.

So sitting in the comfortable salon of *Explorer* it was only to marvel at the travail these men of that era of exploration went through—these stiff English upper-lippers, as a friend of mine put it—and to wonder even why they did such things...this wish to subject oneself to what Apsley Cherry-Garrard had referred to as "the cleanest and most isolated way of having a bad time which has yet been devised."

Often the mental image of men straining in the traces, bent forward into the wind, reminded me of the walking crouch of military troops going over the top in the Ypres Salient, men who had no other choice but to do so. The difference was, of course, that the explorers went on their often death-defying excursions of their own free will. Of the many poems that Shackleton memorized (and quoted) the one that resonates in my mind is by St. John Lucas, containing the line "*But burned with passion for the South | And drank strange frenzy from the wind.*"

"Strange frenzy" indeed.

There are splendid evocations that describe the driving force, that "strange frenzy." One that comes to mind is from Fridtjof Nansen, the

Camp Wild

Tourists in their bright poppy-red float jackets have come ashore on Elephant Island to inspect where Frank Wild and his men awaited rescue. Witness to their arrival are a group of Chinstrap penguins, one of the easiest of the penguins to identify—the thin black line under its chin seems to hold its black cap in place.

Norwegian who was Amundsen's mentor: "An endless procession passes before us—a procession of struggling, frost-covered figures, some erect and powerful, others weak, bent and dying of hunger, cold or scurvy, but all looking forward into the unknown, all gazing beyond the sunset to where their goal might be found … And what were these men seeking? They were setting out with conscious purpose to explore the unknown. In every part of the world and in every age, this quest for knowledge has driven man forward on the path of evolution. And so long as the human ear can listen for the breaking of waves on an unknown shore, so long as the human eye can try to follow the northern lights over silent snowfields, and so long as human thought can reach out toward distant worlds in space, so long will fascination of the unknown carry man ever forward and upward. When man loses this thirst for knowledge he will no longer be man."

Nansen was the explorer who inspired Orde-Lees to volunteer for the Shackleton expedition. Of all the people on the *Endurance*—ridiculed, taunted, referred to as "Peggy," food dropped in his mouth to keep him from snoring—Orde-Lees, I thought, would have looked back upon those years with Shackleton with distaste. Here's how he ends his diary.

"And now to conclude. Is it worth doing? Ask any member of the Imperial Trans-Antarctic Expedition and you will receive the reply, 'Yes I wouldn't have missed it for the world.'

" 'Would you go again?'

" 'Rather! Such is the call of the South!' "

It is a strange impulse. I think I can understand (at least in dramatic fictional terms) the reaction of a man who has had his leg removed by a whale; he wishes to seek revenge. In fact, Melville compares Ahab to the explorers after the Poles as he pores over the charts in his search for the white whale. "He sleeps with clenched hands and wakes with his own bloody nails in his palms … a chasm seemed opening in him, from which forked flames and lightnings shot up, and accursed fiends beckoned him to leap down among them … a wild cry would be heard through the ship … and with glaring eyes Ahab would burst from his stateroom, as though escaping from a bed that was on fire."

How picayune my own quest after the South Georgia pipit, or even the carnivorous duck … the idea of escaping my bunk on *Explorer* as if on fire (either the bunk or me) and rushing into the salon, my startled shipmates looking up from their card games, and shouting at them, "The Georgia pipit! Wilt thou not chase the Georgia Pipit. Art not game for the duck! The carnivorous duck!" etc, etc.

No, of course not. It depends on the majesty of the quest. Shackleton's was the "heroic age of exploration" in which even failure was romanticized.

Fridtjof Nansen (1861-1930)

His return in 1896 after disappearing into the Arctic for three years provided an unforgettable image of the explorer as hero—an inspiration to many, Shackleton included. His two-volume account of his adventures, *Furthest North*, was a further incentive.

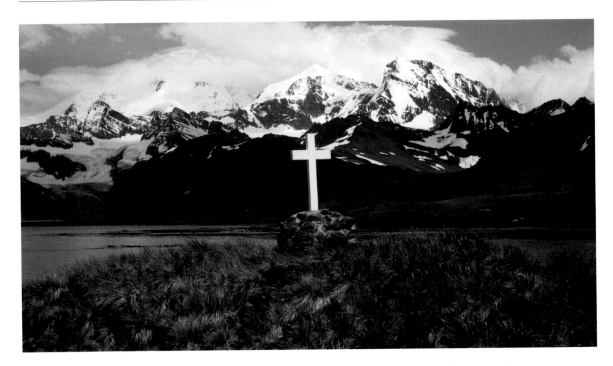

Final Tribute

After meandering about the Southern oceans, including a visit to Elephant Island, the *Quest* returned to Grytviken, where the crew discovered that Shackleton's body had been returned and buried in the whaling cemetery. Nearby, the men of the *Endurance* who were aboard *Quest* had a memorial cairn built, topped with a cross.

Five thousand volunteered to go with him. Reginald James of *Endurance* came because someone he didn't know at Cambridge University yelled out a window as he was passing, "Hey, want to go to the Antarctic?" He replied, "Not particularly. Why?" Apparently the answer was sufficient to get him to sign up.

Some explorers prepared for it in their early, formative years. Amundsen slept in winter with the windows open as part of what he referred to as his "conscious hardening process."

Often the approach is pragmatic. Wilson had written, "Surely God means us to find out all we can of his works." But then when he reaches the Ice Shelf, the *horror vacui*, the horror of emptiness, he mourns, "I am afraid this long southern journey is taking me right away from my proper sphere of work to monotonous hard pulling over an icy desert where we shall see neither beast nor bird, nor life of any kind, and nothing whatever to sketch." And yet, Wilson of all people returns with Scott to the *horror vacui* and eventually to his death on the Shelf.

It was the pain, the suffering that was so hard to comprehend. By comparison I thought of the space explorers leaning back in what looked like lounge chairs, speaking through their helmets to someone in Houston, Texas, as if they were involved in doing nothing more dangerous than sitting in the rear of a bus. The prick of a meteorite could end all that very quickly, but it had none of the long drawn-out agonies of the people in the Antarctic snows. Compare Apsley Cherry-Garrard: "Such extremity of suffering cannot be measured: Madness or death may give relief. But this I know: We on this journey were already beginning to think of death as a friend. As we groped our way back that night, sleepless, icy and dog-tired in the dark and the wind and the drift, a crevasse seemed almost a friendly gift."

And what kept them from the kind of surrender to "the friendly gift" that finally overwhelmed Captain Oates ("I am just going outside and I may be some time")? Something, I would presume, on the order of Winston Churchill's admonition, "Once you get to hell, keep on going."

Or Lord Tennyson's line picked for the cross piece erected by the men who brought back news that Scott had perished: "To strive, to seek, to find, and not to yield."

Perhaps it was something else. Frank Wild of *Endurance* speaks of the Antarctic with a curious image: "After you have seen the white unknown you can never escape the little voices."

They can't seem to help it. A phrase from the Koran comes to mind: *That which God writes on thy forehead, thou wilt come to it.*

So as I sat in the comfort of the *Explorer's* salon with my gin rickey I began thinking of the images that my trip to the Antarctic had left me with——the strange brooding silence of the deserted whaling stations, the way the wind moved across the pale green of the tussock, the fluttery flight of the pipit, of course, the mountain climbers drifting out to sea on a floe down the Lemaire channel, Elephant Island's bleak, shingled beach, Frank Hurley's photograph of *Endurance's* tangled rigging and the slant of her funnel, black against the snow, as she settled in the Weddell sea with the soccer games within yards, the mountains rising out of their reflections on water as if from a mirror, the gentle waves that rocked the Zodiac from a whale that had breached across the cove, and yet of all this it was the little graveyard at Grytviken that was the most pronounced in mind: The dark mountains rise so steeply behind it that they seem almost threatening, an overhang of rock. Indeed, back in the whaling ship days an avalanche came out of them while a station manager was walking along the water's edge and took him with it out into Cumberland Bay.

We grouped in our red parkas around the tall stone of Shackleton's grave, and pictures were taken. The murmured voices gave a kind of animated existence to a place which, once we had trooped down to the Zodiacs to return to the *Explorer*, must surely be one of the loneliest graveyards on earth.

And yet the final, somewhat mocking, image which came to mind was this: The South Pole is now marked with a metal sign planted deep in the snow. Each year the ice sheet above it moves three yards. So at New Years, the Americans who maintain the outpost place a metal stick at the pole's exact spot. The marker sticks of past years, three yards apart, stretch far into the distance…

✧ ✧ ✧

Moving Marker

Since the ice mass moves about thirty feet in the direction of 43 degrees west annually, a geographic pole marker about thirteen feet long is pounded two thirds of its length into the snow every year, at a brief Pole-moving ceremony. At this rate the flags placed by Amundsen on December 14, 1911 and then Scott on January 17, 1912 will drop into the Southern oceans in about 120,000 years.

Photo Credits

Page #/ Position	Credit	Page #/ Position	Credit	Page #/ Position	Credit
1	Royal Geographical Society	33	Bettmann/Corbis	62	Reproduced by permission of the Scott Polar Research Institute
2-3	Corbis	34 (top)	Bettmann/Corbis		
4-5	Paul A. Souders/Corbis	34 (bottom)	Bettmann/Corbis		
6	Royal Geographical Society	35	Hulton-Deutsch Collection/Corbis	63	Galen Rowell/Corbis
7	Bettmann/Corbis	36	Michael Nicholson/Corbis	64	Reproduced by permission of the Scott Polar Research Institute
8	Wolfgang Kaehler/Corbis	37	Bettmann/Corbis		
9	Greg W. Lasley	38	Hulton Archive/Getty Images	65	Reproduced by permission of the Scott Polar Research Institute
10-11	Wolfgang Kaehler/Corbis	39	George D. Lepp/Corbis		
12	Reproduced by permission of the Scott Polar Research Institute	40-41	Ann Hawthorne/Corbis	66	Bettmann/Corbis
		42	Royal Geographical Society	67	Galen Rowell/Corbis
13	Hulton-Deutsch Collection/Corbis	43	Galen Rowell/Corbis	68	Reproduced by permission of the Scott Polar Research Institute
14	Bettmann/Corbis	44	Reuters NewMedia Inc./Corbis		
15	John Conrad/Corbis	45	Hulton-Deutsch Collection/Corbis	69	Reproduced by permission of the Scott Polar Research Institute
16	Hulton-Deutsch Collection/Corbis	46-47	Reproduced by permission of the Scott Polar Research Institute		
17	Hulton Archive/Getty Images			70	Reproduced by permission of the Scott Polar Research Institute
18	Hulton Archive/Getty Images	48-49	Bettmann/Corbis		
19	Hulton Archive/Getty Images	50	Bettmann/Corbis	71	Reproduced by permission of the Scott Polar Research Institute
20	Peter Johnson/Corbis	51	Hulton Archive/Getty Images		
21	AFP/Corbis	52	Bettmann/Corbis	72	Reproduced by permission of the Scott Polar Research Institute
22	Pat & Rosemarie Keough	53	Peter Johnson/Corbis		
23	Corbis	54	AFP/Corbis	73	Reproduced by permission of the Scott Polar Research Institute
24-25	Hulton-Deutsch Collection/Corbis	55	Hulton-Deutsch Collection/Corbis		
26	Bettmann/Corbis	56	Dave G. Houser/Corbis	74	Underwood & Underwood/Corbis
27	Royal Geographical Society	57	Martin B. Withers; Frank Lane Picture Agency/Corbis	75	Reproduced by permission of the Scott Polar Research Institute
28-29	Hulton Archive/Getty Images	58	Reproduced by permission of the Scott Polar Research Institute		
30	Royalty-Free/Corbis	59	Paul A. Souders/Corbis		
31	Bettmann/Corbis	60-61	Underwood & Underwood/Corbis		
32 (top)	Hulton Archive/Getty Images				
32 (bottom)	Bettmann/Corbis				

Page #/ Position	Credit	Page #/ Position	Credit	Page #/ Position	Credit
76	Underwood & Underwood/Corbis	105	Wolfgang Kaehler/Corbis	132	Pat & Rosemarie Keough
77	Galen Rowell/Corbis	106	Paul A. Souders/Corbis	133	Pat & Rosemarie Keough
78	Peter Johnson/Corbis	107	Pat & Rosemarie Keough	134	AFP/Corbis
79	Greg W. Lasley	108	Galen Rowell/Corbis	135	Morton Beebe/Corbis
80	Underwood & Underwood/Corbis	109	Greg W. Lasley	136	Ann Hawthorne/Corbis
81	Hulton-Deutsch Collection/Corbis	110-111	Wolfgang Kaehler/Corbis	137	Morton Beebe/Corbis
82-83	Galen Rowell/Corbis	112-113	Reproduced by permission of the Scott Polar Research Institute	138	Bettmann/Corbis
84-85	Reproduced by permission of the Scott Polar Research Institute			139	Bettmann/Corbis
				140-141	Hulton-Deutsch Collection/Corbis
86	Pat & Rosemarie Keough	114 (top)	National Maritime Museum	142	Underwood & Underwood/Corbis
87	Reproduced by permission of the Scott Polar Research Institute	114 (bottom)	Royal Geographical Society	142-143	Hulton-Deutsch Collection/Corbis
		115	Royal Geographical Society	144	Ann Hawthorne/Corbis
88-89	Reproduced by permission of the Scott Polar Research Institute	116	Reproduced by permission of the Scott Polar Research Institute	145	Hulton-Deutsch Collection/Corbis
				146	Hulton-Deutsch Collection/Corbis
90	Bettmann/Corbis	117	Pat & Rosemarie Keough	147	Bettmann/Corbis
91	Reproduced by permission of the Scott Polar Research Institute	118	Pat & Rosemarie Keough	148	Wolfgang Kaehler/Corbis
		119	Bettmann/Corbis	149	Hulton Archive/Getty Images
92	Reproduced by permission of the Scott Polar Research Institute	120-121	Reproduced by permission of the Scott Polar Research Institute	150	John Noble/Corbis
				151	Galen Rowell/Corbis
93	Royalty-Free/Corbis	122	Reproduced by permission of the Scott Polar Research Institute		
94	Peter Johnson/Corbis				
95	Pat & Rosemarie Keough	123	Dave G. Houser/Corbis		
96	Courtesy of the Nantucket Historical Association, GPN4448	124-125	Royal Geographical Society		
		126	Bettmann/Corbis		
97	Pat & Rosemarie Keough	127	Hulton-Deutsch Collection/Corbis		
98-99	Graham Neden; Ecoscene/Corbis	128-129	Royal Geographical Society		
100	Bettmann/Corbis	129	Digital image 1996 CORBIS; Original image courtesy of NASA/Corbis		
101	Paul A. Souders/Corbis				
102	Bettmann/Corbis				
103	Paul A. Souders/Corbis				
104-105	Pat & Rosemarie Keough	130	Galen Rowell/Corbis		
		131	Galen Rowell/Corbis		

Additional Captions

pg. 1: A windproof burberry-cloth hood worn by Ernest Shackleton on the 1907–1909 *Nimrod* Expedition.

pg. 2: A photo by expedition photographer Frank Hurley shows the *Endurance* trapped in the ice of the Weddell Sea in 1915.

pg. 3–4: An abandoned whaling station at Leith Harbor, South Georgia Island.

pg. 10–11: The bow of the *Explorer* cuts through floating ice in the waters off Antarctica. One of the best places to enjoy the Antarctic scenery is from the bow, especially when going through icebergs known as "growlers" for the sound they make as they scrape along the ship's side.

pg. 28–29: A watercolor by expedition artist George Marston depicts the *Nimrod* cutting through the pack ice on its way to McMurdo Sound.

pg. 46–47: Before the *Endurance* left South Georgia for Antarctica, Frank Hurley scaled a peak to take this panoramic photo of Grytviken Harbor and the surrounding mountains and glaciers.

pg. 60–61: One of the icebound *Endurance*'s crew brings food to the dogs, which were kept in "dogloos" on the ice alongside the ship.

pg. 88–89: Launching the *James Caird* on April 24, 1916, to begin the journey to South Georgia Island.

pg. 98–99: This mountain range on the Antarctic continent was named for Shackleton—a fitting tribute to the first man to conquer the equally rugged mountains of South Georgia Island.

pg. 110–111: Cape Lookout on Elephant Island.

pg. 124–125: The deck of the *Aurora*, sheathed in ice and snow.

pg. 139-140: Shackleton waves goodbye as he sets out on the *Quest* in 1921.

Notes to William Logan's Poem *Endurance*

1. British explorer Sir John Franklin, who disappeared with two ships and 128 men after sailing into the Arctic region in 1845 in search of a Northwest Passage between the Atlantic and Pacific oceans. Franklin's ships, *Erebus* and *Terror*, had previously been commanded by Sir James Ross in the Antarctic. The public fascination with Franklin's fate and the many expeditions sent in search of him marked the start of the so-called "Heroic Age" of polar exploration. The Northwest Passage was ultimately conquered by Roald Amundsen, who sailed through it aboard the small vessel *Gjoa* between 1903 and 1906.

2. British explorer Henry Hudson, who sailed closest to the North Pole of anyone in his era. Hudson died in 1611 with his young son, in a small boat set adrift by mutineers in the bay that bears his name.

3. British naval officer William Bligh, who in 1789 was set adrift in the South Pacific after the famous mutiny aboard the *Bounty*. His successful open-boat voyage to the East Indies has been compared to Shackleton's trip on the *James Caird*.

Index

A

Adams, Jameson Boyd, 42, 45
aerial photographs, 19
albatross, 9, 18, 51, 53, 93, 109
Alexander, Caroline, 6–7, 69, 71
Amundsen, Roald, 6, 32–33, 42, 50,
 144, 149–51
reaching South Pole, 48–50
Andersen, Matthias, 105
Anker, Conrad, 100
Antarctic, 13
Antarctic Convergence, 30
Antarctica, 13–14
 first aerial photographs, 19
 lure of, 31, 123, 143, 145, 148–51
Arnesen, Liv, 144
Artuso, Felix, 108
Aurora expedition, 55, 125–127,
 129–36, 141
austral summer, 66

B

Baines, Bob, 39, 107, 133
Baines, Christine, 39
Bakewell, William, 87
Banks, Joseph, 31
Barrie, J. M., 51
Barrill, Ed, 33
Beardmore, Elspeth, 63
Beardmore, William, 37, 63
Beardmore Glacier, 44, 50, 54–55,
 63, 129
Belgica, 32
Bennett, Floyd, 65
birds, 7–8, 19–20, 30, 53, 58–59, 149
 albatross, 9, 18, 51, 53
 King Penguins, 56
 skua, 117
 South Georgia pipit, 109
 striated caracara, 20
Blackborrow, Percy, 7, 57–58, 68, 70
 frostbite, 84, 86, 114, 146
Bligh, William, 68, 96
blizzards/white-out, 129, 130
Bonner (seaman), 18

Borchgrevink, Carsten, 13, 18–19
"Boss, the." *See* Shackleton,
 Ernest Henry
Bounty, 96
Bowers, Henry, 6, 7, 50, 52, 126
Brocklehurst, Philip, 43
Browning, Robert, 23, 108
Butler, George, 8
Byrd, Richard, 50, 65, 66, 129

C

Caird, James, 54
Camp Bloody Wild/Cape Wild, 89,
 117–19, 148
Campbell, Joseph, 39
Campbell, Victor L., 90
Cape Evans, 126–27, 129–32, 134, 136
Cape Rosa, 63
Cape Royds Hut, 21, 40
Cape Wild/Camp Bloody Wild, 89,
 117–19, 148
Cecil, Lord Robert, 142
Charcot, Jean-Baptiste, 31, 41,
 132–33
Chase, Owen, 96
Cherry-Garrard, Apsley, 11, 81, 87,
 129, 143, 148, 150
Chetwynd, Rosalind, 63
Churchill, Winston, 37, 54–55, 69,
 119, 142, 151
Clark, Robert, 64, 87
clothing, 81
Coffin, Hezekiah, 96
Coffin, Owen, 96
Coleridge, Samuel Taylor, 18
"Colonel." *See* Orde-Lees,
 Thomas Hans
Cook, Frederick, 32, 48
Cook, James, 13, 26, 31, 32, 56
Crean, Tom, 65, 74, 91, 99, 101–102,
 122

D

Daisy, 105
Dance, Nathaniel, 13

Darwin, Charles, 23
Davis, John King, 135
Dawson-Lambton, Elizabeth, 63
de Gerlache, Adrien, 32
Deception Island, 78–79, 121
depots, food, 55, 126, 129, 135, 144
Discovery expedition, 6, 15–21,
 23–27, 41
 conditions, 11, 20–21
 diet, 24–26
 entertainments, 23
Docker, Dudley, 54
dogs in polar expedition, 20–21, 25,
 49, 60, 65, 77
Donaldson, Isobel, 63
Dorman, Emily. *See* Shackleton,
 Emily (nee. Dorman)
Dudley Docker, 75, 84–85, 91, 111, 121

E

Elephant Island, 86–87, 89–90,
 111–15, 119, 121–23
Eliot, T. S., 102
Emanuel, Victor, 30
Emma, 121
"End, The," 74
Endurance expedition, 53–55, 57, 61,
 135–36, 143. See also *Aurora*
 expedition; *James Caird* expedition
 abandoning ship, 71–75
 conditions, 62
 crew photos, 116, 122 (*See also*
 individual names of crew members)
 diet, 70, 77, 80–81, 85
Elephant Island, 86–87, 89–90,
 111–15, 119, 121
entertainments, 58, 62, 64–65, 68,
 79–80, 115–16
 King Haakon Bay, 94–99, 119
 later speculations, 138
 mountain crossing, 99, 101–102
 Patience Camp, 75–77, 79–87
 rescue missions, 119–21, 134–35
 South Georgia Island, 57–58
 Weddell Sea, 71, 83
Endurance (poem), 9

Endurance (ship), 62, 69, 71
Erebus, 34
Essex, 96
Evans, Edgar, 6, 7, 50
Evans, Frederick Pryce, 45
Everett, F. W., 35
Explorer, 39, 94, 105, 132
Explorer tour, 8–9, 11, 147–48
 Albatross Island, 58–59
 Deception Island/swimming,
 78–79
 Elephant Island, 117–19
 Falklands, 17, 19–20
 Petermann Island, 132, 133–34
 Shag Rocks, 29–30
 South Georgia Island, 56–57,
 102–103, 105
 Stromness/Grytviken, 106–108
 Weddell Sea, 65–68

F

Falklands, 17, 19–20
Ferrar, Hartley, 20
Fisher, James, 115, 142
Flintshire, 15
Foca 1. See *Quest*
food depots, 55, 126, 129, 135, 144
fourth man, 102
Fram, 49, 68–69
Français, 31, 132
Frolich, Theodor, 26
Frost, Robert, 145
Fuchs, Arved, 144
Fuchs, Sir Vivian, 135–137, 138
Fuchs-Hillary Expedition, 136–138
Furthest North, 47, 68
Furthest North (book), 149
Furthest South, 24, 25, 44, 47, 129

G

Gadded, John and Carol, 39
Gaze, Irvine, 129
geographic pole marker, 151
George, David Lloyd, 54
Glasgow, 121

"Great Glacier." *See* Beardmore
 Glacier
Green, Charles, 70, 115, 145
Green, Reginald, 80

Green Album, 74, 77
Greenstreet, Lionel, 84–85, 87,
 114–15
Grytviken, 58, 61, 102, 105, 107–108,
 146–47
 funeral church and grave,
 107–108, 150, 151
Guinness, Edward, 38, 54

H

Hadley, John, 93
Hayward, Vic, 125, 129–33
Heart of the Antarctic, 47, 143
Hillary, Sir Edmund, 135–37, 138
Hoghton Tower, 12
Holl, William II, 13
Holness, Ernest, 82
Holst, Axel, 26
"hoosh," 21, 77
How, Walter, 76, 87
Hudson, Hubert T., 58
humidity, 81
Huntford, Roland, 9, 15
Hurley, Frank, 7, 58, 62, 64–65,
 68–69, 100, 112–13
 abandoning *Endurance,* 72, 74–77,
 151
 Elephant Island, 111, 114–17,
 121–23
 Patience Camp, 79–82, 84–87
Hussey, Leonard, 61, 68–69, 79,
 143
 abandoning *Endurance,* 74
 Elephant Island, 114, 122
 Quest, 141, 145–46
Hut, Cape Royds, 21, 40
hut, refuge, 133
Hut, the (Scott's), 19
Hut Point, 126, 129–31
Huxley, Thomas, 23

I

ice field/pack ice, 19, 62, 73, 80, 83
icebergs, 30, 71, 83, 112
Imperial Trans-Antarctic Expedition.
 See *Endurance* expedition
Instituto de Pesca No 1, 121
Italia, 50

J

Jackson, Frederick, 42
James, Reginald, 62, 72, 76, 86, 115,
 150
James Caird expedition, 7–8, 75, 80, 82,
 89, 91–97, 119–21
 photographs of, 84–85, 100
Jason, 118
"Johnny Rook," 20
Joyce, Ernest, 125–26, 129–32, 135

K

Kagge, Erling, 144
Kapitan Dranitsyn, 8
katabatics/winds, 129
Kerr, Alfred, 87, 145
King Haakon Bay, 94–99, 119
King Penguins, 56
Koonya, 38
Kristensen, Leonard, 13

L

Larsen, Carl Anton, 107, 118
Lasley, Greg, 19–20
Lay Sermons, 23
Leslie, Sir Shane, 142
Lind, James, 26
Lindquist, Frans Wilhelm, 23
Lipton, Sir Thomas, 37
"Little Red Ship," 8. See also *Explorer*
living conditions, 11, 20–21, 44,
 92–95, 111, 114–16, 131
Logan, William, 9
Loken, Pastor, 108
Los Angeles (plane), 79
lure of adventure, 31, 123, 143, 145,
 148–51

M

Mackay, A. F., 45
Mackintosh, Aeneas, 125–26, 129–33
Macklin, Alexander, 74, 77, 115, 122,
 141, 146–47
Mallory, George, 100
Markham, Sir Clements, 15, 53
Marshall, Eric, 42–43, 45
Marston, George, 55, 91, 115, 121
Mauger (carpenter), 141

Mawson, Douglas, 42, 45
McCarthy, Tim, 91, 97, 119, 141
McGillan (stoker), 45
McIlroy, James, 62, 114–15, 141–42, 146
McLeod, Thomas, 146
McMurdo Sound, 18–19, 27, 41, 125, 127, 132–35, 137–38
McNeish, Harry, 64–65, 68, 71, 80, 99, 101, 146
 clash with Shackleton, 75–76, 91
 James Caird, 91, 94
 Peggotty Camp, 97, 119
Mellor, Frank (Shackleton's brother), 36–37
Melville, Herman, 59, 96, 149
Messner, Reinhold, 100, 144
Mill, Hugh Robert, 16, 35
Moby Dick, 59, 96 more
Monmouthshire, 12
morale. See *specific expeditions*
Morning, 27
Mount Donaldson, 63
Mount Erebus, 43
Mount Rosa, 63
Mrs. Chippy (book), 6, 69
Mrs. Chippy (cat), 6–7, 58, 74, 146

N

Nansen, Fridtjof, 47, 68, 148–49
National Arctic Expedition. See *Discovery* expedition
navigation, 93–94, 99
Neptune's Bellows, 78–79
Nimrod expedition, 21, 38–45, 125, 143
Nobile, Umberto, 50
Nordenskjold, Otto, 19, 81
Norge, 50
nunatak, 21

O

Oates, Laurence, 6, 7, 126, 151
"Old Lady." See Orde-Lees, Thomas Hans
Orde-Lees, Thomas Hans ("Colonel," "Old Lady," "Peggy"), 62, 64, 68–71, 91–92, 113–14, 147, 149
 Dudley Docker, 84–85

Elephant Islands rescue, 121, 123
 Patience Camp, 75, 77, 87
Origin of Species, 23

P

pack ice/ice field, 19, 62, 73, 80, 83
Patience Camp, 75–77, 79–87
Peary, Robert, 33, 48
Peggotty Camp, 97, 119
"Peggy." See Orde-Lees, Thomas Hans
penguins, 56, 86, 105, 148
Petermann Island, 132, 133–34
Plimpton, George, 6–8, 9
poems, 9, 145
Polar Medal, 76, 146
polar winter, 44
Polaris, 55
Pollard, George, 96
ponies in polar expeditions, 42–44
Pourquoi Pas?, 132–33
Priestley, Raymond, 90
primus stove, 23
Princess Anne, 134
Professor Gravel, 147
Pynchon, Thomas, 31

Q

Quest expedition, 140, 141, 143, 145–46, 150

R

Raymond, 39
Richard, R. W., 22
Richards, Dick, 125–26, 129–32, 134
Rickenson, Louis, 87, 115
Rime of the Ancient Mariner, 18
"Road Not Taken," 145
rogue waves, 94–95
Rosa Lind, 63
Ross, Sir James, 22, 34, 43
Ross Ice Shelf, 6, 18–19, 21–22, 135, 137–38, 150
Ross Ice Shelf Party, 128, 129–36
Ross Island, 126–27
Rowett, John Quiller, 143
Royal Navy officers, 90

S

Safety Camp, 126, 129
Samson, 119
Sante Fe, 108
Saunders, Edward, 143
scientific exploration, 37, 50–51
Scott, Robert Falcon, 6, 11–12, 15–16, 37, 90, 125, 130, 136
 Discovery expedition, 18–21, 23–27, 41
 grave, 52
 last expedition, 48–51, 126, 150–51
 photographs of, 7, 16, 81
scurvy, 24, 26
seal skinning, 115
seals, 56–57, 62, 103, 105, 106, 115, 117–18
Service, Robert W., 145
sextant, 93
Shackleton, 9, 15
Shackleton, Edward (Lord), 15
Shackleton, Emily (daughter), 15
Shackleton, Emily (nee. Dorman), 15, 23, 27, 34–35, 48, 143, 147
Shackleton, Ernest Henry ("the Boss")
 background/character of, 12, 15–17, 34–37, 47–48, 54, 64, 142–43
 funeral church and grave, 107, 108, 147, 150
 health, 24–25, 43, 141–42, 146–47
 Murmansk, 142–43
 photographs of, 6, 15, 17, 33, 35, 37, 45, 140, 142
 photographs of with crew, 55, 76, 80, 87
Shackleton, Frank (Mellor), 36–37
Shackleton, Raymond, 15
Shackleton's Antarctic Adventure, 8
Shackleton's Great Boat Journey, 90–92
Shag Rocks, 29–30
Shaw, George Bernard, 11
Sir Ernest Shackleton, 100
skua, 117
snow blindness, 24
Snuggery, the, 111, 114, 121–22
South, 9, 74, 76, 93, 121, 143
South Georgia Island, 7, 9, 56–58, 147

South Georgia pipit, 109
South Polar Times, 34
South Pole, 42
South Pole, reaching the, 48–50
Spencer-Smith, Reverend Arnold
 Patrick, 125, 129–31
St. John Lucas, 145, 148
Stancomb Wills, 84–85, 86, 91, 111
Stancomb-Wills, Janet, 54, 63, 143
Stenhouse, John, 127
striated caracara, 20
Stromness Bay, 59, 101, 102–107, 119
summer, austral, 66
supplies/equipment, 99, 136–39. *See
 also specific expeditions*
swimming, 79

T

Tennyson, Lord, 151
Terra Nova expedition, 27, 90, 130, 134
Terror, 34
Thomas, Lowell, 79
Tom Crean, 100
Trip (tour leader), 109
Tunzleman, Alexander, 13

tussock/tussock nest, 9, 20, 103, 105
Two Brothers, 96

V

Venables, Stephen, 100
Vicars, Sir Arthur, 36
Vincent, John, 91, 92, 97, 119
Vinson, Carl G., 14
Vinson Massif (mountain peak), 14
von Bellinghausen, Fabian, 13
von Spee, Graf, 121
Voyage of the Discovery, 37

W

Waste Land, 102
whaler's church, 107
whales, 118
whaling communities, old, 104, 106
white-out/blizzards, 129, 130
Wild, Ernest, 125–26, 129–31, 141
Wild, Frank, 18, 42, 44–45, 54, 57, 91,
 125, 129–30, 141
 Elephant Island, 111, 114–16,
 121–22, 148

Endurance sinking, 71, 77
 photographs of, 45, 76, 87
 Quest, 146, 151
Wilkins, Hubert, 79
Wilson, Edward ("Bill," "Uncle
 Bill"), 6, 7, 20–21, 23–25, 34, 38,
 126
 grave, 52
 Ross Ice shelf, 50–51, 150
winds/katabatics, 129
winter, polar, 44
Wordie, James, 64, 87
Worsley, Frank, 62, 65, 141
 Endurance sinking, 71–72
 James Caird, 75, 89–94
 mountain crossing, 97, 99,
 101–102, 105–106, 119
 Patience Camp, 77, 85
 Quest, 146
 Yelcho rescue, 122
Worst Journey in the World, 11, 87

Y

Yelcho, 118, 121–23

Acknowledgements

The publishers would like to thank A&E Networks, Avalon Publishing Group, and their associates for their hard work and good humor throughout this project. Special thanks go to Max Alexander, Tracy Armstead, and Lisa Vaughn-Soraghan for efforts above and beyond the call of duty, and to Sean Moore, f-stop fitzgerald, and Will Balliett for their vision in conceiving this series and their determination to make it a reality. We would also like to extend our continued appreciation to ColourScan Ltd., Singapore, for their excellent work.

Avalon Publishing Group would like to thank Jonathan Gregg, Joshua Mehigan, Craig Colligan, and Judith Josvai for their efforts on this project, as well as the kind cooperation of Hilary Johnston at TimePix, Yvette Reyes at AP Wide World Photo, Colombe Meurin at Photos12.com, and Valerie Zars at Hulton Getty. At DK, Chuck Lang for his support; Chuck Wills for his dogged pursuit of accuracy and good writing; Dirk Kaufman for his great design eye, and Gregor Hall for keeping things moving with patience and understanding. At AETN, Juan Davila, Chey Blake, Charles Wright, Liz Durkin, and David Walmsley all helped put the pieces together, Cindy Berenson kept the ball rolling with her grateful professionalism and, most of all, thanks to Carrie Trimmer, who has supported this series and has contributed to it in so many ways above and beyond the call.

Author's Acknowledgments

O ne of the memorable moments on my trip was when the *Explorer* passed the Russian icebreaker *Kapitan Dranitsyn* near Elephant Island. I was called to the bridge and on ship-to-ship radio found myself talking with my old friend George Butler, who after a moment passed me on to Jonathan Shackleton, a second cousin of the explorer. I wondered instantly if his voice matched his forebear's—thus the illusion of talking to the "Boss" himself. I thanked him, rather clumsily, for a relative whose life had drawn me to visit the seas he had first sailed almost a century ago.

So he is on my list. So are George Butler and Caroline Alexander, who provided me with material from their extensive library; Geoffrey and Jorie Kent, for granting me passage on the *Explorer*. What friends they have been over the years! And Rosemarie and Pat Keough, whose limited-edition *Antarctica* is a superb collection of photographs taken over two austral summers. I owe so much to Will Balliett and Max Alexander, my editors at Avalon, for their encouragement and help.

The literature on polar exploration is vast. The following books on the Antarctic were of particular value to me: Leonard Bickel's *Shackleton's Forgotten Men* (a splendid account of the *Aurora* and the Ross Ice Shelf expedition), Michael Smith's *An Unsung Hero, Tom Crean—Antarctic Survivor*, David G. Campbell's *The Crystal Desert*, Ian Cameron's *Antarctica, The Last Continent*, Caroline Alexander's *Endurance* (as well as *Mrs. Chippy*), Susan Solomon's *The Coldest March*, the invaluable Lonely Planet publication, *Antarctica*, and above all Roland Huntford's remarkable and monumental biography, *Shackleton*. His sources include 173 *books* (I counted), one entitled *Parachuting and Skydiving* by T.W. Willans—I would guess to check on Orde-Lees' parachute jump from the Tower Bridge.

As I mention in the foreword, everyone on the expeditions of the time kept journals; many wrote books—Shackleton, Cherry-Garrard, Scott, Hurley, Hussey, Wild, Worsley, and some of them had books written *about* them. I am grateful

The Author

Sitting with merry friends in a Zodiac, I have no idea why I look so gloomy. Possibly my Wellington boots contain two or three cupfuls of ice water from a misstep while going ashore, or perhaps I fear another confrontation with a fur seal. Whatever, that aspect by no means suggests my feelings about the expedition. I cannot imagine having a better or more instructive experience.

Dinner Jackets

The Adélie penguin, here on Devil Island in the Weddell Sea, has a solid black head with a white eye ring and most satisfies the image of the penguin as a gentleman (small) in a tuxedo. It is also the most numerous of the penguins—a colony at Camp Crozier at the edge of the Ross Sea contains as many as 200,000 birds.

to New York's Explorer's Club, whose library and its considerable shelf of exploration literature of this nature was of great use.

I would have written much more about my fellow passengers, whose splendid company I will remember and covet, if it weren't for the necessity of concentrating on the Shackleton expeditions. As for Abercrombie & Kent leaders aboard, their knowledge about the Antarctic as we heard from their lectures and their competency in every aspect of our experience was outstanding. They include Trip Dennis, the expedition leader, whose Actors' Studio voice over the ship's intercom got us going every morning; the cruise director, Geraldine Massyn, and the assistant cruise director, Sally Millns; the naturalists and lecturers include Barry Albright, Chris Cutler, Ingrid Nixon, Charley Wheatley, Kevin Clement, Ralph Eshelman, Gillian Walker, as well as my friend Greg Lasley from Victor Emanuel Nature Tours, who every evening in the salon went over the day's checklist with those who had signed on for the bird watching.

And especially to Ingrid Nixon and Kevin Clement. They decided to get married during the trip and indeed took advantage of Captain Uli Demel's ability to officiate at the exchange of vows and marry them at sea. Champagne afterwards. A grand way to end the trip.

—George Plimpton